CONTENTS

Cameroon
on a
Clear Day

by

Helga Bender Henry

William Carey Library
Pasadena, California

Published by
William Carey Library
P.O. Box 40129
Pasadena, California 91114
(818) 798-0819

Library of Congress Cataloging-in-Publication Data

Henry, Helga Bender, 1915—
    Cameroon on a Clear Day / Helga Bender Henry
        p. cm.
    Includes bibliographical references and index.
    ISBN 0-87808-293-X (alk. paper)
    1. Bender, Carl Jacob, 1869-1935.   2. Mis-
sionaries—   Cameroon—Biography.   3. Missionaries—United
    States—Biography.   4. North American Baptist
    Conference—Clergy—Biography.   I. Title.
BV3625.C23B464   1999
266'.61'092—dc21
[b]   99-13355
                                                        CIP

ILLUSTRATIONS

FOREWORD

What significance can one man—only five feet five inches tall and weighing but 110 pounds, and given almost as much to poetry and art as to theology—possibly have had for a time of tumult much like ours? Why would a lad virtually a teenager leave Germany for life and citizenship in America and then close his eyes to the fabulous "American dream" and reverse his life course to cast his fortunes instead among native Africans?

Carl Jacob Bender's name permeates the Christian missionary story in Cameroon, West Africa, from the beginning of our century throughout a generation in which he, like few others, found a revealing window on a barren and needy spiritual field. Among the natives of Cameroon he probed traditional rivalries, viewed critically the implications of colonialism for the big banana and cocoa plantations, noted the duplicity of West African slave trade, and lived and labored throughout World War I amid the struggle for supremacy between England, France, and Germany. But above all else he was a career missionary sharing with others the incomparable gospel of Jesus Christ.

Because Bender hoisted an otherwise unused American flag over his mission complex, he virtually held invading forces at bay, and after a furlough returned in the post-War era to build the Soppo headquarters church and its adjacent educational and recuperation facilities, only to fall victim himself to black water fever virtually on the eve of his scheduled return to America.

The story of the Benders' missionary trials and triumphs is told here by Helga Bender Henry, the last of the six children born to Carl and Hedwig Bender. When British military forces sought during World War I to evict or imprison all missionary personnel, the Benders protectively lofted the American colors. They remained in Cameroon for five years without external monetary support while they encouraged native believers spiritually and kept careful records of Cameroon Christian enterprises, irrespective of denominational sponsorship. All conversation and correspondence was interrupted between members of the family, the children being separated like orphans in Berlin with little word of their parents or news of a baby sister's birth.

This chronicle of the Benders sheds light on the twentieth century's early efforts to evangelize Cameroon during the first two decades or so. Helga Bender, born in Soppo, I met first in America in the mid-1930s when we were students at Wheaton College. Neither of us had a calling as career missionaries, but we had missionary hearts that beat for Christian world-witness.

Helga's professional competence was attested, as both *Who's Who in America* and *Who's Who in American Education* indicate, by completion of Bachelor of Arts, Master of Arts in Education, and Master of Religious Education degrees. Her skills were facilitated by post-graduate linguistic studies at George Washington University. Her ability in German, which she taught at the collegiate level in Wheaton and in Ellendale State Normal School where she was dean of women, was excellent background for translating volumes written in German by her missionary-pioneering father, as well as German materials prepared by others. She taught at Northern Baptist Theological Seminary and at Eastern Baptist Theological Seminary, was associate professor of education at Pasadena College, and wrote Christian education materials and Sunday School lessons. Her comprehensive interest in evangelism is evidenced by her translation for the 1966 World Congress on Evangelism in West Berlin of Paulus Scharpff's *History of Evangelism* and her authorship of the volume titled *Mission on Main Street*.

By insisting on original sources rather than relying on oral tradition, the narrative serves a somewhat corrective role. There is nothing, for example, to confirm a report that military authorities banned Bender from Soppo for writing a libelous book against the government and summoned him to stand trial before an international court. The rumor may have been a distorted account of the Benders' brief detention in Duala in an effort to confine all missionary holdouts. Bender was not uncritical of government, but he was not anti-government.

Extensive research was completed on materials for this volume at the Hamburg Baptist Seminary archives in Germany, where records were available that had been stored underground during World War I to escape destruction during military conflict. Other research was done at the Basel Mission archives in Switzerland, the School of Oriental and African Studies of the University of London and the Friends House Library also in London, and at the British Museum. Additionally there were two extended visits in Paris to the Bibliothèque Nationale, and in the United States to Princeton University library and the archives of the North American Baptist Seminary in Sioux Falls, South Dakota.

In addition materials were researched and gathered during a two-week visit to Cameroon in 1963, where at a reception Helga was welcomed to the Soppo Church by women from some twenty congregations that had been nurtured into existence by the original Soppo church. In addition I had a trip to Christian campuses in Africa under the auspices of ACTEA in 1982, during which, as ACTEA lecturer, I had opportunity to pursue numerous interviews with informed Cameroonians. Helga has meanwhile kept in touch periodically with the Cameroon ambassador and with friends and associates knowledgeable about the Cameroon scene.

This volume is much more than a reflection of the early rise of Christianity among the Bakwiri and other Cameroon tribes, although its historical interest eliminates some missing links and supplements others. By no means is it a comprehensive history, for the story of early Cameroon missions includes many missionary volunteers, among them some who served well and in not a few instances even gave their lives on the field.

This account sheds light on various noteworthy aspects of missiology, often presenting a contrast with more recent alternatives. It reflects a distinctive philosophy of missions, one which, while Baptist in emphasis, included well before our time an interest also in ecumenical Christianity and social and cultural concerns and differences as well. It did so without obscuring the centrality of the gospel, the indispensability of evangelism, and the necessity for religious education. The missionary agenda was not merely a matter of periodic preaching services; it included one-on-one conversations with a genuine interest in the problems and perplexities of the natives and their contrary worldviews.

The Bible, as Bender taught it, was the supreme book

of life, and it presupposed the living God in contrast with pagan conceptions of the supernatural. It required translation, and translation prepared the way for hymn-writing and hymn-singing expressive of the joy that Christianity nurtures in heralding the salvific death of Jesus Christ, and his bodily resurrection and prospective triumphant return. These realities Bender considered essential to church planting and church renewal.

Bender's message included a concern for both justice and mercy. His interest in human rights was evidenced by his insistence that American citizenship needed to be respected by invading powers. The gospel he preached was not "a white man's gospel"; it was *good news* no less for blacks and others. Bender's attitude toward colonialism was critical of exploitation of labor by plantation owners. But he also recognized new opportunities afforded natives, while deploring vices accommodated and even nurtured by some international trading enterprises.

Yet Bender was more interested in persons than in movements and institutions. Individuals were not reducible to statistics and summary. He and humans of whatever race were part of an extended family—not in theory only but in practice also, as when he invited a native to share his lodgings. He joined in meals served from a common pot, and was not taken aback when his serving included a choice monkey hand.

Bender knew that missionary success does not depend on size and stature; his own was diminutive. But he trusted God's providence, which he well knew called at times for one's supreme sacrifice. He was large in the love of God and man, and this love carried him to the so-called 'dark continent' where the gospel shed light on the human predicament and offered hope unparalleled.

Carl F. H. Henry

Map of pre-war workfields in German Kamerun (Cameroon)

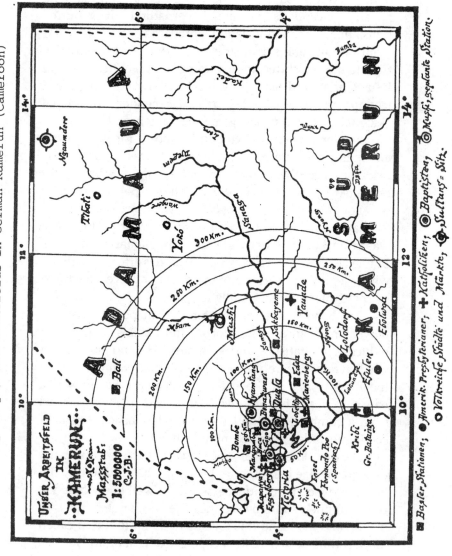

PREFACE

Cameroon on a Clear Day is the story of a teenager who with his family emigrated from Germany to the United States in 1881. While working as a department store clerk, he was led to Christ by a fellow worker, attended a dynamic church where the Gospel was proclaimed, and experienced a call to foreign missionary service. In due course he attended seminary, became an American citizen, and in 1899 became a missionary pioneer in West Africa. On his first furlough he met a devout young woman in Germany who secretly had a call to Cameroon missions. She soon became his missionary wife. Of the 150 missionaries in Cameroon by World War I, the Benders virtually alone were not exiled or imprisoned by British and French troops.

This book portrays also Bender's final return (1932–1935) to Cameroon where in 1935—just weeks before his planned retirement—he was completing work on the steeple of the newly built Soppo church, when he slipped and fell. When growing weakness led to black water fever he died and was buried in a gravesite thereafter dedicated to the memory of the Cameroonians' beloved *Sango*.

When missionary biographers narrate the spiritual fortunes of Cameroon they specially mention Carl Jacob

Bender (1869–1935), always with respect and on occasion also with awe. In many respects a model missions worker, he labored often from dawn to midnight charting the next plateau of his pioneering ministry.

To help escape deportation or imprisonment by invading British and French forces, Bender, as already indicated, courageously hoisted an American flag over his West African compound. Because the Benders held American citizenship they alone among German missionaries could remain in Cameroon during World War I. When they went on furlough in 1919, the entire mission field was confidently left in indigenous native hands except for Paris Mission engagement.

Separated during the tumultuous War years from his Berlin-reared children, deprived of any regular salary, and surviving on a native diet, Bender and his wife patrolled as best they could the fields left behind by retreating Catholic, Lutheran, Presbyterian, and fellow Baptist workers, many of them sent to Fernando Po and still others to Spain, France, England, and Germany.

In the historical overview *Heritage and Ministry of the North American Baptist Conference* (Oakbrook Terrace, North American Baptist Conference, 1979), Frank H. Woyke comments that Bender "proved himself to be both a beloved missionary and a keen student of the land, its people and their culture" (p.216). Alongside vigorous evangelistic engagement he promoted also improved medical resources, mission hospital care, and the need for nurses.

In *The New International Dictionary of the Christian Church* (ed. J. D. Douglas, Zondervan, 1974) the historian Richard V. Pierard tributes Bender's development of more than two dozen outstations in ten years, and establishment of both a school and a missionary rest center in Soppo.

The comprehensive *Biographical Dictionary of Christian Missions* (ed. Gerald H. Anderson, Simon & Schuster Macmillan, 1998) in a significant sketch specially notes Bender's effective pioneer work near Duala prior to his relocation at Soppo and then in the interior in evangelism, educational work, and scientific research. Pierard, contributor of the article, notably comments that Bender "became an advocate for the Africans." He notes that, although he lacked formal anthropological training, Bender had "great appreciation" for African culture, published ethnological books, and through his schools "contextualized the Christian message and developed an effective indigenous ministry."

In his book *International Influences and Baptist Mission in West Cameroon* (E. J. Brill, 1993), Charles W. Weber writes that first among three key German Baptist missionaries in Cameroon—Carl Bender, Paul Gebauer, and George Dunger—Bender showed great respect for African culture. Yet Bender espoused a somewhat different approach to African culture, evangelism, and the role of education and mission strategy (p.28). Bender decried the cultural perspectives of colonial government and the encroachment of Western culture on indigenous African societies (p.43). Yet he viewed African culture as itself in a process of deterioration to which colonial regimes themselves contributed. The real need of Africa, he stressed, lay in more vigorous evangelism by trained native evangelists, educational programming, care for the sick and suffering, and enlistment of Cameroonian young people in missions.

Bender sought to train national leadership that would be self-supportive. Inexperienced missionaries grievously err, he held, if in the absence of an awareness of the Africans' outlook on life, African Christians are approached as if they were merely European congregations. Bender thus advocated contextualization of the gospel message, and opposed an imposition of European forms on Africans. For him an ultimate goal of education is Christian character development.

Central among Bender's emphases were evangelism and education, understanding the indigenous culture, training Cameroonian leadership for churches and schools, church planting that radiates from a main station, self-sustaining churches, and personal example of dedication and hard work. An indefatigable yet highly practical administrator, he was respected by nationals, government officials and agents, missionaries of whatever affiliation, and even by merchants and traders who disdained missionaries in general, yet considered him competent, compassionate and genuine—a model of missionary presence and momentum.

Helga Bender Henry

ACKNOWLEDGMENTS

This book represents the supportive interests and prayers of many people and organizations in many countries. In our almost fifteen years of international travel, people of different tribes and nations have enriched our sense of both relationship to one another and of mutual responsibility in Kingdom work. Helpful people everywhere are well-remembered; many of them continue to be good correspondents. Fortunately they recognize the impossibility of, nor would they think necessary, the public mention of their names. Several have included references to the Benders in their books; some have suggested or loaned helpful books even of their own; and some have occasionally administered slap-on-the-back encouragement.

Family members and relatives including son Congressman Paul Henry, now with the Lord, have patiently encouraged this project. Their willingness to accept extensive family absenteeism merits recognition. Fortunately, daughter Carol Henry Bates, researcher and published writer of harpsichord and other musicological materials, and I could dove-tail travel and archival procedures. Her proficiency in French and mine in German encouraged good cooperation in both our projects. Our shared appeal to God and thanksgiving for his daily care of family and ourselves and progress in our daily work was spiritually sustaining and rewarding.

To go and tell, go and show, and especially go and love, as did the Benders in Cameroon, can remove, for us, too, barriers of ignorance and indifference that hinder perception, let alone participation in Christian enterprise. We thank those who financially support mission work in Cameroon and elsewhere. Even more we are thankful for the consistent and knowledgeable prayers for awareness of world mission. Proper recognition and reward for helping share God's saving grace among lost and seeking mankind is of course beyond this world's self-aggrandizing interest or ability to give. Nonetheless, ready obedience to the Savior's daily prompting to do what we can yields incomparable joy and blessing.

We are surrounded in our country with millions of international students and families, some of them in our towns and cities, who could become important links in God's work. I remember one perceptive foreigner who, when encountered by someone's rush-by "How are ya?" indicated "I never had a chance to say." That Bender every day at a given time sat at a well-known spot along Soppo road to meet, befriend, and help passersby was part of his well-remembered and fruitful ministry.

A final thanksgiving I offer to Esaso Wolete and Sarah, both now in heaven. Meeting me and my husband at Tiko Airport, Missionary Kwast drove us on what was but a bush path in Bender's day, and later a place of encampment for British troops outside Soppo mission station, and stopped abruptly to greet Esaso, lugging on his shoulder a large stalk of bananas. It was Esaso who in Bender days carried me on his shoulders to protect me from lurking animals or other dangers. For verification of identity we addressed each other in German, English, and

Duala and happily rejoiced in this reunion.

At a welcome coffee several days later Sarah, then president of the Women's Society but once just a small child loved and spiritually nurtured by Hedwig Bender, greeted me. Offering me on behalf of her people and for them an expensive gift of fresh eggs, she said just a few words, more significant and eloquent than she probably realized. "We thank the Lord," she said, "that he has brought you safely home."

To God indeed and alone be the glory. To others—families, many fellow workers, and worldwide brethren in Christ—be joyful thanksgiving that by his grace we can wend pilgrim pathways together from earth's temporary housings to claim our reserved abodes.

1
ONCKEN

Hamburg, Germany, had been a participant in early Hanseatic trading when countries like England, France, Holland, and others plied the seas to make, develop, or commercialize colonies and protectorates. Being a relative latecomer to such expansionism, Hamburg on the Elbe River nonetheless outwitted England, as it were, in its 1884 snatching of agreements from Duala kings to occupy and take charge of extensive Kamerun River territory. It was actually Hamburg shipping merchants like Woermann Company who prepared for and implemented this takeover. Its representatives remained highly active and visible in Kamerun affairs until World War I and resumed thereafter during mandate years.

Bandied about principally by alternative power struggles especially between Lutherans and Catholics who held its citizenry in check, Hamburg finally granted freedom of worship and of civil rights to all of its people after the War of Liberation and its eventual new constitution of 1860.

Resident in the city long before such liberalization was John Oncken. Born near Bremen in 1800, but already by 1814 located in Scotland, he became apprenticed for several years to a Scottish but London-based merchant. Converted there through the ministry of thriving independent religious groups like the Continental Society, Oncken returned to Hamburg in 1823 as an evangelist of that organization.

He brought back with him among other things London-learned experiences of Sunday Schools, use of religious literature, social outreach to the poor and needy, and the practice of meetings and fellowship in Christian homes. His prompt carryover of such ministries to Hamburg occasioned repeated resistance and imprisonment of Oncken but to no avail. Numbers of unreached or church-dissatisfied people by their increasing attendance encouraged Oncken and his co-workers to continue their work whatever the political or civic penalties might be.

Opposition turned to acceptance and even support of Oncken when Hamburg was almost destroyed by fire. The prompt supply by Oncken's people of food, clothing, and shelter in Christ's name to homeless and helpless but still inimical citizens became a humanitarian bridge of undeniable love and caring. From then on Oncken and his followers were welcomed and respected as citizens worthy of full acceptance and proper recognition.

When severe winter froze in a merchant vessel from the United States, its captain rejoiced to find the Oncken people a haven of personal and spiritual blessing. He in fact promised to inform his American Baptist friends and church officials about people in Hamburg who seemed ready on the basis of the New Testament study to accept the tenet of believer's baptism by immersion.

Early in summer a young New York Baptist theology teacher, Barnas Sears, en route to graduate studies in Germany arrived in Hamburg. During his visit he,

Oncken, and six others gathered at night on the far shore of Hamburg's Elbe River for a baptismal service. Before he left, Sears, also in the name and authority of his American Baptist church, ordained John Oncken and even incorporated the Hamburg assembly as a valid Baptist church.

This event of believer's immersion baptism, the first of its kind in Germany, now became a practice throughout Germany and other European countries as well. Oncken himself journeyed to many locations to immerse believers, or candidates traveled to Hamburg for the ritual. As Baptists emigrated to the United States many of them did so with the blessing of Oncken's ministry to them and as ambassadors of a growing Baptist influence.

Another Hamburg development was an association of Baptist leaders who gathered periodically from various locations to discuss denominational trends and concerns. In view of missionary strides being made by American Baptists in India, China and elsewhere, the question arose whether the Baptists in Germany should follow suit. Two opinions kept vying for resolution. Some leaders approved sending funds to and by way of already established mission societies like the American Baptist. Others felt the time was ripe for a new German Baptist home-grown and home-directed mission society.

Philip Bickel, first graduate of Rochester Theological Seminary, who for many years worked in both American and German sponsored enterprises before returning to Hamburg to assist in Oncken's publishing enterprise, staunchly supported the former. Eduard Scheve, progressive pastor in Berlin, supported the latter, and in time would organize a Missions Committee as a step toward the eventual organization of a legally approved denominational missions society. The earliest missionaries to Kamerun were processed through Scheve's committee.

Because of his remarkable influence throughout Europe, Oncken came to be called "The Apostle of the Continent." In 1857 Charles Spurgeon, whom Oncken had heard preach in London and had come to know, arrived in Hamburg to dedicate a new chapel for him. Visitors from many parts of Europe as well as from the United States came to participate in this event and in a related preaching conference that featured the two men. Memorial cup trophies were available, one of which can be viewed at Spurgeon's London College. It reminds viewers not only of a dedicatory occasion in Hamburg, but also of two renowned ambassadors for Christ and their shared passion for extending God's kingdom worldwide.

Contributing to the realization of that passion was the founding in 1880 of the Hamburg German Baptist Seminary. Among its supporters and leaders was Gottlob Fetzer, who, like Philip Bickel, after a stint in the United States had returned to Germany to help develop denominational projects overseas. Several early missionaries for Kamerun trained at Hamburg Seminary and were commissioned there. Of great value at the seminary are official archives that were safely buried underground during World War I and represent a major repository of books and papers useful for research. Berlin, unfortunately, lost many if not most of its materials to military attacks.

Hamburg has maintained its importance for denominational growth and progress. Significant as was its commercial power in the takeover in 1884 of what became Kamerun, no less significant is its modeling of tenacity for implanting and nourishing spiritual power to the ends of the earth.

2
IMMIGRATION 1881

According to family records Carl Bender's forebears arrived in Germany by way of France. Here about 300 years ago they helped establish Eschelbach, a hamlet near Heidelberg in the duchy of Baden, a small state along the Rhine River. Constantly overrun by different armies during years of both religious and political strife, this region would rock back and forth between French and German occupation. In due course, as a member of Napoleon's Confederation of the Rhine, the now Grand Duchy Baden would eventually undergo still further re-identification as the western part of Baden-Württemberg in today's Federal Republic of Germany. The Benders survived these early uncertain political times, not to mention the series of devastating plagues that claimed millions of lives across Europe and almost wiped out Eschelbach.

The original Eschelbach home, a half-timbered stone structure, served successive families and generations. Its oversized kitchen with large hearth and oven, and harboring also the customary spinning wheel of those times, provided food, fellowship, and constructive busyness. In an adjacent room stood a seven-foot loom on which several generations, including that of Bender's father, wove green flax.

Behind the house a large barn, sheltered by a gentle hill, housed cows, goats, geese, and chickens. At the front flowed a small brook that nurtured fruit and walnut trees and fragrant roses. The seeds of Bender's later Kamerun gardening, botanical, and landscaping interests, were probably sown here in this scenic village. Acreage on the town's outskirts, subdivided among the villagers, supplied vegetables and grains of many kinds for food and barter, and flax as well.

Perhaps Bender's grand- or great-grandfather had learned and practiced weaving in France before the move to Eschelbach, Germany, his father's birthplace. Perhaps here as his father's first-born, Carl learned to cultivate and care for flax plantlets that grew an inch a day for thirty to forty days before ripening for hand-picking and pre-loom preparation. An additional bonus on each stem would be its lovely blue flower-crown whose seeds were pressed into linseed oil. Required in all aspects of even these early childhood years were strong backs, willing hands and purposeful determination, and parental obedience.

The Eschelbach Benders no doubt boasted a long lineage of weavers; here in their small village, however, George Michael was the only such artisan whose children hopefully would in turn continue the family cottage industry. Besides helping with flax cultivation Carl also already helped fill spools for his father's loom.

Carl's school teacher foresaw—at least hoped for— something quite different for his bright student's future. When he offered to provide higher education for the lad, and at no cost, weaver Bender's refusal was not atypical of the times: a child must not rise above the station of his parents, lest he in time become ashamed of home and family. Several years later, in America, circumstances and perspectives would settle the matter of the future for both father George Michael Bender and all his children.

Meantime in Eschelbach parents and children met each day's procedures and requirements in traditional well-ordered and orderly German style. Thus Carl and his eventual four siblings learned the "hows" of daily living, but no less the "whys" and wherefores" that nurtured moral and practical readiness for eventual independence and decision-making.

With increasing numbers of Germans in the 1800s, a Bender uncle had emigrated to the Unites States; periodically he urged the Eschelbach kin to join him there. Not until long after his service in the Franco-Prussian War (1870–1871), however, would George Michael Bender respond to the overseas invitation.

In 1881, after a two-week stormy ocean voyage from Bremen, George Michael Bender, wife Fredericka, and children Carl Jacob, Susan Christine, Frieda, Helena, and George arrived in New York to settle in Buffalo. That particular time in the annals of immigration was fortuitous in a way; it was the last opportunity for relatively easy entry to America through what was then called Castle Garden. The Ellis Island complex, with its regulations and for many years trying situations, would open in 1892.

During the 1880s alone over 356,000 immigrants entered New York at Castle Garden. Assigned there by the Baptist General Missionary Society to assist especially, but not only, German immigrants—perhaps the Benders, too—John Schiek during his tenure helped over 7,000 newcomers. He made house calls at immigrant hotels, visited the sick in hospitals, conducted religious services, and distributed Bibles, Christian periodicals, and tracts

(25,200 in nine different languages). He also furnished maps to churches.

Built by the federal government in 1807 the pre-Ellis compound was first named Castle Clinton to honor New York's then governor, DeWitt Clinton. Ceded in the 1820s, however, from federal to New York City local control, the structure and area were soon leased to private interests for an amusement center and renamed Castle Garden. Here in what became a fashionable and popular venue for many artists, world-acclaimed Swedish opera star Jenny Lind in 1850 made her American debut.

Nonetheless, a further development for Castle Garden came in 1855 because of New York City's changing composition. That year it became the first official receiving station that offered unwary immigrants basic protection from interlopers and provided valid information about transportation, money exchange, location of relatives, and so on.

Until 1892 most immigrants, like the Benders, entered North America directly through New York with little or no hindrance, although ports in other states were similarly available without difficulty to continuing masses of arrivals. The industrial depression in Germany in the 1880s had led to a large exodus of skilled craftsmen, among them weavers, spinners, glass workers, and leather workers. Overall until 1895 the northern countries of Ireland, Germany, Britain, and Scandinavia had dominated immigration to the United States. Between 1890 and 1914 fifteen million immigrants would come from southern and eastern Europe.

Already by 1812 almost 250,000 Germans had settled in the American colonies, coming usually as entire families to seek and embrace religious, economic, social, and political freedoms and opportunities unavailable in sometimes starving enclaves of European overpopulation. Later even Kamerun, like the United States, was perceived as a possible outlet and haven for crowded Germans.

In areas expanding through German concentrations of eager and active citizens, the United States came to be envisioned as a "New Germany" of independent republics; among such settlements was Wisconsin, the most German of all the states. Congress quashed these ideas, however, recognizing the need to lessen feelings of what came to be called hyphenism, that is, a lingering dualism of political and personal loyalty. By World War I, German-Americanism had accordingly moved from acceptance and tolerance of hyphenism to its disapproval and actual disallowance. Hyphenates were out; full-blown Americans were in.

Arriving in the United States in 1881 at age 12, Carl Bender during his lifetime would experience much of this and later historical transition. The uncle who had emigrated previously and was an already established farmer in Folsomdale, New York, promptly took Carl and sister Susan into his family for two years of basic American orientation. On rejoining his family in Buffalo, New York, at age 14, where his grandparents now had also settled, Bender was quite ready perhaps to continue school but also to seek employment, a word of special significance to newcomers even if of uncertain definition and realization. In Hengerer's large department store, Carl became a "bundle boy," soon to be promoted, however, to clerk in fabrics and dry goods, a position he maintained for ten years until his departure in 1893 for Rochester Seminary. In those early days everyone worked ten hours a day, six days a week, for $6.00 to $9.00 a week and pooled income for family maintenance. On Saturdays all stores were open until 10 p.m.

Before long, Carl Bender's Sunday hours would also be preempted. An alert colleague at Hengerer's Department Store invited him to church services. Bender's inherited German state-imposed Lutheranism was respectable, predictable, and familiar in its routines. What he now encountered in accepting his friend's invitation was certainly something new. This "other church" offered a spontaneous voluntarism, joy and enthusiasm of involvement and fellowship, plus biblical sharing and exposition that he before had never experienced. Together with sister Susan who like him would later minister in Africa, he was soon converted to a mature and personal faith in Christ, received immersion baptism, and joined the Third Street Baptist Church, one of Buffalo's already then three German Baptist congregations.

There his prompt involvement in church life and activities helped fashion essential preparation, even if presently unrecognized by him, for Rochester Seminary and beyond that, for Kamerun. Together with other young men he regularly shared in house visitation, street meetings, tract distribution, and community aid endeavors. Even being pelted with eggs or vegetables now and then was a foretaste of yet other things to come in future times and places. Determination grew to serve God, whatever the cost. That cost included adequate training. Bender therefore in 1893 at age twenty-four bade farewell to the chapter of ten years in Hengerer's Department Store.

3
SEMINARY

By the mid-1800s German Baptists in the United States already had twenty-five churches, within a decade, seventy-three, and by another decade, one hundred thirty-eight, with 10,809 members. The need for trained pastors and for more churches was unmistakable.

When American Baptists, largely from Rochester, New York, in 1830 established a new university in Rochester that included a theological seminary department, Zenos Freeman, Secretary of the Baptist Union, in 1851 promptly encouraged Germans to attend for ministerial training. The first catalogue offered a four-year course of both collegiate and theological subjects. One German responded that year. The first actual graduate, however, was Philip Bickel.

Disappointed by the failed 1848 Revolution in Germany, Bickel fled to America. Arriving in Waukegan, Illinois, and there helped to conversion by a Methodist pastor, he was immersed in Lake Michigan by a Baptist minister. Before long Bickel enrolled at Rochester. Not only was his command of English more than adequate but—to help meet seminary expenses—he tutored ambitious students in French and/or German. Of his French tutees, he later married Catherine Clarke, of highly-placed Pilgrim heritage. Graduated in 1855 Bickel soon became prominent among both American and German Baptist administrative, missionary, and publication ventures. He returned to Germany in 1878, there in Kassell to direct Oncken's publishing and book enterprise.

At Rochester ever-zealous Zenos Freeman had anticipated a possible language problem for most early German students. "There's a danger," he said, "lest these men pursue studies too much under instructors who are *not* German; interest and fluency in the German language and the power to use it fluently might be lost" (a lostness that later in World War I years would be encouraged). Needed, Freeman emphasized, in this formative period, was someone to head the university's German department seminary "who will give thorough instruction to prepare preachers among the Germans."

Seminary authorities therefore secured August Rauschenbusch as full-time professor for the Germans. Highly educated in Europe, Rauschenbusch had in 1846 emigrated to America, soon becoming a bilingual itinerant pastor, worker for the American Tract Society, Baptist affiliate, and denominational leader. For thirty-two years, from 1858 until 1890, Rauschenbusch invested his abilities and energies for training pastors and missionaries for German Baptist ministries at home and abroad.

He had come to Rochester with interesting and significant credentials. After university he had succeeded his father as pastor in a large Lutheran church, but at age thirty emigrated to Missouri where, having witnessed immersion baptism of an acquaintance and recognizing the validity thereof, he decided to follow this course for himself. He was immersed in the Mississippi River in 1850. Thereafter he helped establish German Baptist churches until he accepted the opportunity and invitation of the

New York Baptist Union to teach at Rochester Seminary. During his thirty-two years, one hundred ninety men came under his tutelage; one hundred seventy-seven entered the ministry and remained thus till their deaths.

Enrolling at Rochester in 1893, Bender missed direct classroom experience under this remarkable spiritual and educational giant. He did, however, study under Herman Schaeffer, pastor of the First Baptist Church in New York City, who in 1872 had come to the seminary to teach and to assist Rauschenbusch. Energetic and far-sighted he secured a five-story building that would accommodate seventy residential students, offer lecture rooms, a chapel and whatever other facilities were needed for a school's more independent existence and operation. Here in the so-called "Students' Home," Bender and fellow students slept, ate, studied, worshipped, and struggled for up to six years to complete their training. Extended fellowship among and with both students and faculty became unforgettably real and durable. Bender not only attended classes and worship services, but also worked in the laundry, kitchen, did cleaning, gardening, and other tasks to cover expenses. Bonus money at times came through his poetry-on-order requested by lovelorn but inarticulate comrades. Poems that verbalized his own emotions and experiences were of a different kind. These he systematically recorded in a diary-type folio begun already in pre-Rochester days and augmented through most of his life and that included details of time, place, and circumstance of writing. It is virtually an autobiography in verse form of a remarkable servant of God.

Writing assigned essays and sermons at Rochester—carefully read and evaluated—helped sharpen Bender's literary pursuits. Later in Kamerun he wrote teacher training materials in the Duala language as well as correspondence with natives. In America later, he wrote Sunday school lessons in both German and English for denominational publications like *Der Sendbote*, and issued publications mentioned elsewhere in this book. He often illustrated his books and articles and also drew maps as needed. Good writing together with painting and sketching were special activities that later he helped nurture among his children. In his stateside pastorates he painted baptismal scenes as backgrounds for special services.

Bender's favorite professor was J. D. Gubelmann, experienced pastor, administrator, and missions enthusiast. Among his earliest assigned responsibilities was to personally interview and examine would-be seminary students. In the classroom he was thorough in presentation, strict in assignment implementation, and exacting in evaluation of submitted materials. Under him Bender studied homiletics and sermon preparation. Times of counsel were meaningful and to the point, and in Bender's case, helpful in terms of orientation for missions.

One further professor was Walter Rauschenbusch, son of August, who like his father came with outstanding educational credentials that in time were employed in both the English and German departments of Rochester University. His emphasis on what came to be known as the social gospel was born in large part during his pastorate among the poor and suffering fringe of society housed in the slums of New York City and often exploited by industrial tycoons. His interests in anthropology and its significance for ministerial and missionary work, together with a firm conviction as to the nature of sin and the need for redemption became significant and well-received for many years and far beyond any particular denomination. He and other younger professors coming into the seminary picture would help usher in a new period of its history.

Walter Rauschenbusch had been a student under Dr. Augustus Hopkins Strong, president of Rochester University. Born in Rochester in 1836, son of a wealthy newspaper man and brother of the founder and president of Eastman Kodak Company he moved in socially and professionally influential circles. Converted under the preaching of Charles Finney while a student at Yale, Strong completed college, seminary, and other studies in Berlin, then pastored several churches, and was soon to be acclaimed for his spiritual ardor and expositional gifts. He served as president and professor of systematic theology at Rochester University and Seminary from 1872-1912.

His nurturing of interdenominational associations of varying theological persuasions soon gathered around him friends called "New Theologians"and those of more conservative stance called "Strong's Boys." He became well-known for his daily chapel Bible studies that modelled some of the spiritual and practical dimensions he sought to nurture in his students and would-be Kingdom workers. He became as it were a pastor of pastors-to-be and those already pastors-in-fact.

Although himself committed to historic Reformed theology, this perhaps most notable North American Baptist theologian of the nineteenth and early twentieth centuries kept himself and his students alert to growing philosophical and hermeneutical changes. Still remembered even today in some circles is his three-volume *Systematic Theology*. In this work Strong exposed perhaps thousands of seminarians and pastors to rigorous examination and evaluation of biblical truth. Bender himself burned and burned out many a lamp in poring over Strong's *Systematic Theology*. Later writings reflected Strong's honest wrestling with the impact of developing science on creationism, for example, on divine immanence, divine transcendence, and inevitably, divine revelation and scriptural authority. Scholars' active attempts to reconcile God's "truth once delivered" with human philosophical and scientific wanderings and wonderings, or their disengagement from such efforts, resulted in biblical, theological, and educational rifts current even today.

During the same time span another development would be a part of Bender's important exposures. In 1886 Chicago evangelist Dwight L. Moody invited 251 students from eighty-seven American and Canadian colleges for several weeks of Bible study and prayer at Mount Hermon, Massachusetts. During that time no one even mentioned the word "missions." It was the surprise arrival of Moody's friend A. T. Pierson that seemed to spark what became a virtual conflagration. Presbyterian pastor, writer, lecturer, and itinerant missionary, his word that "all should go and go to all as a matter of supreme loyalty to Jesus Christ" helped broach the subject. Several Princeton, Harvard, and Oberlin students had been praying for such a break, one that set the stage for the subsequent "Meetings of the Ten Nations."

In brief speeches three sons of missionaries in China, India, and Persia, followed by a Dane, a Norwegian, an American Indian, a Japanese, a Siamese, a German, and an American appealed for volunteers to "go into all the world." In closing, all ten speakers repeated "God is love" in their particular native language. A visitor just returned from mission experience in China exhorted the young people to understand missions "as a war of conquest, and not as a mere wrecking expedition."By the close of this first Mt. Hermon Conference the number of already committed mission volunteers increased from twenty-one to exactly one hundred, leaving one hundred fifty-one delegates to grapple with later decision-making.

Before returning to their campuses, the conferees organized themselves into an official movement. Certain obvious leaders were approved for visiting yet uninvolved continent-wide and even international campuses to spread the word and challenge of "The Student Volunteer Movement for Foreign Missions." Five years later in 1891 at the first international Convention in Cleveland, Ohio, it was reported that over 6,000 men and women had enlisted as volunteers from three hundred fifty institutions. Each of these enlistees had voiced the consecratory statement, "We are willing and desirous, God permitting, to become foreign missionaries." John R. Mott and Robert Wilder would become committed leaders of this movement and in time would be involved in the Edinburgh Mission Conference of 1910 and subsequent post-World War I situations and developments. The movement's purpose, "Evangelization of the world in this generation," was not to mean "the conversion, or the Christianization, or the civilization of the world...." It was to mean, rather, that the Christians of this generation are to "give every person of this age an opportunity to accept Jesus Christ."

The excitement of the Student Movement penetrated Rochester Seminary no less than other schools. Several students undoubtedly influenced by it carved pioneer steps as well as pioneer graves into Kamerun soil. The reality of these facts would overtake Bender soon enough.

The year 1899 was not just another year, certainly not for Carl Bender, who a few months after graduation would himself embark for West Africa. Nor was it just the end of another century, one whose residues of disaster but also of hope lingered in peoples' and nations' memories. In moving the clock to 1900, the fading year of 1899 set in

motion what would remain of the twentieth century. This
turn from past to present brought hints and promises of
constructive nationalism from monarchism, liberation
from static dependency, and social democracy from blatant
oppression. Repositioning breezes of religious and political
freedom refreshed vision and purpose for humanity.

Since arriving in America in 1881 and during his
Rochester Seminary years (1893–1899) Bender had
witnessed and shared in the astonishing growth of
American communities, establishment of both secular and
religious institutions, emergence of public and
denominational leaders and expansion of
humanitarianism. As an immigrant he had accepted and
learned to personally emulate proffered benefits of his
new homeland. His work in Kamerun would continue for
him and in turn demonstrate to generations of receptive
Africans the sometimes difficult modus operandi of
graciously receiving for purposes of selflessly sharing.

Graduated from Rochester German Baptist Seminary
in 1899, Bender needed two additional qualifications for
ministry: ordination and American citizenship. These
"rites of passage" materialized in Buffalo, New York, his
home base since coming to America.

The Third Street Baptist Church, of which Bender was
a member when he left for seminary, was not the first
Baptist church established in that city. Actually the
Germans in time had five churches there, all of them
growing directly or indirectly from the Washington Street
Baptist Church founded in 1848 by Alexander von
Puttkamer.

Not born until 1869 nor emigrated from Germany
until 1881, Bender would not have known this pastor. His
special name would not be forgotten, however, since a
relative, Jesko von Puttkamer, governor of Kamerun from

1895 to 1907, would be a neighbor in his specially built "castle" in capitol city Buea, near the Soppo Baptist Mission. Bender and Jesko von Puttkamer would know each other.

His relative, Alexander von Puttkamer, had wearied of serving in the Kaiser's private military guard and opted for an escape to America. Arriving in New York in 1836, he was converted in 1837 in Lawrenceville, New York, and there joined an English-speaking Baptist church. The Prussian von Puttkamers were apparently not unaware of non-Lutheran and non-Catholic religious movements. Alexander's niece, Johanna von Puttkamer, was the wife of Bismarck. Brought up in pietistic teaching she faithfully exhorted her husband toward Christian commitment, but to little avail. Her uncle's religious odyssey in the United States, however, may have had earlier Separatist influences, like that of Johanna.

In any case, Alexander von Puttkamer soon became a colporteur for the American Tract Society and later a missionary of the American Baptist Publication Society, assignments that brought him to Buffalo and its German community. Here with nine of his converts and several others he founded the 1848 church, and pastored there until 1852. He established and pastored other churches as well, even in Wisconsin (near Watertown), then part of the American Western frontier.

Von Puttkamer's abilities and energies joined those of August Rauschenbusch and two others who in 1851 formed in Philadelphia the first German Baptist local association known as "Conference of Ministers and Helpers of German Churches of baptized Christians, usually called Baptists."

By 1853 von Puttkamer had also organized a church in Albany, New York, there to pastor until leaving to serve in the Civil War, first "as regimental chaplain, then as captain of artillery...." Among the battles in which he fought was the Battle of Chancellorsville, where his beloved commander General Whipple was killed.

After the War he pastored English churches exclusively and attended his American wife of forty-two years through a three-year illness until her death. Now, for the first time since 1835, von Puttkamer returned to his German birthplace. He was heartbroken by his relatives' disinterest in his American experiences. In fact, during his stay in the United States, unknown to Alexander, his family had revoked his legitimate inheritance.

Nonetheless, for him the greatest of all benefits, not only for now, but for all eternity, remained his matchless inheritance in Christ. He died on March 2, 1893, at age eighty-six, at the Baptist Ministers Home in West Farms, New York.

The 1894 *Baptist Annual* of the New York State Missionary Convention called Alexander von Puttkamer "thrice a nobleman—by birth, by nature and by grace. His life marked an era. He was the first German to be baptized by an American Baptist minister; the first (German) to be ordained in our (American) communion; he also organized the first German Baptist Church in New York (Buffalo) ... the first of its kind in America." The *New York Tribune* obituary called him "a milestone in the road of religious progress." As Bender eventually moved about in ministries, he, like many others, could have been a legatee of Alexander von Puttkamer's presence and influence for Christ and his Kingdom in Buffalo and elsewhere.

In May, 1899, besides ordination under Buffalo pastors, Bender also met his need for American citizenship. Such identification would authenticate— especially in 1914—his declared right to remain in

Kamerun throughout and beyond World War I. At that time naturalization procedures were state-regulated. Bender therefore appeared before a New York judge, verified his command of English, proved United States residence of at least five years, attested conditions for financial stability, and took an oath of allegiance to the flag. He wore his subsequent certification of American citizenship like a second skin that protected and spoke for Bender throughout many years' travels and challenges.

Carl Jacob Bender

4
KAMERUN (1899–1903)

In October 1899 Bender went joyfully to undertake his missionary task, one full of surprises. Whatever conditions and circumstances faced him in Kamerun, he nonetheless never regretted his call as a missionary. Having crossed the Atlantic, he boarded a passenger ship for Duala, one of West Africa's busiest seaports and at that time the main mission station of German Baptists.

Arriving with Bender were two young women also traveling to the Kamerun field, Dorothy Karls and Frieda Lutz. After the customary stop en route at Teneriffe and Madeira, the ship steamed into Victoria Harbor, where a group of Independent Baptists (a spinoff from Saker's early work) heralded the arrivals and wished them Godspeed to Duala, five hours distant.

Duala was the German government's Kamerun headquarters and the most active seaport on the west coast. At the end of a four-week trip from Europe it was an enticing sight. Small coast guard cutters transferred the passengers from anchorage in the high seas to canoes that then took them to various points of call, including eventually the Duala Mission Station. Fortunately, the tide was in, or the arrivals would have had to trek laboriously through the sand or be carried by natives.

All available workers gathered to welcome the new recruits. For a few months of orientation Bender was promptly assigned to the boys' boarding school, which trained natives for future Christian teaching activities. He was learning Duala, the main language of the west coast blacks, and he was designated to do visitation work at the two dozen mission outstations in the Duala country.

Bender traveled with an older colleague to various stations to familiarize himself with the country and its people, and to learn firsthand their customs and practices. He was welcomed not alone by church members but by natives generally. In the villages everyone wanted to see and shake the hand of the "New White One." Children were curious, and women brought their babies to be held by him. He was welcomed as a guest by tribal chiefs and by church members who sang hymns at his arrival.

He was then assigned to Bonakwase, a main station on the Kamerun river a day's journey from Duala by canoe. Before the end of 1901 he was very much alone in his mission, which centered in Aboland but extended also to the entire territory of the Ewori River and a part of Bassaland as far as Nyamtang. His preaching circuit and visitation usually took two to three weeks, for which he took necessary clothing and a minimum of food.

These were still Bender's bachelor days. In Aboland he learned to cook for himself, as well as to do laundry as he had in seminary days to pay expenses, until he could teach Johann, his youthful aide, to take over such chores.

One of Bender's converts in Aboland in 1900 was twelve-year-old Otto Epale of the Abo tribe, whom Bender taught in Sunday school and in 1901 baptized at Bonakwase. After his conversion Epale studied at the boys' boarding school in Duala and at age fifteen began teaching in his home district.

Bender had made it a goal from the first to be at home with the natives, visiting in their huts and eating with them. He mentally closed his eyes to filth and uncleanliness, eating like his hosts by dipping with his fingers into the common pot.

One of his first culinary surprises came while sharing a common stew from which he drew a well-cooked monkey hand. On another occasion Bender was invited for chicken dinner and was assured it would be ready in thirty minutes, when indeed it was attractively served on a banana leaf. But, remarked Bender, "the chicken hasn't been dressed." "We'll take care of that right now," said the host, as he eviscerated the innards.

One day one of the boy helpers at Bender's hut caught a horned viper which, when dissected, disgorged a two-pound bushrat; the natives promptly devoured both creatures. Not long thereafter a python, caught menacing the chicken coop, was shown to have swallowed five chickens, and the natives fully enjoyed the combination.

On one occasion at Bonakwase in Aboland, Bender introduced Western fare as a lure to get together Priso and Ngo, two furiously feuding chiefs. The German government had declared Ngo chief, but the natives on the whole regarded Priso to be the real chief because he resisted colonial regulations. A police expedition had burned down Priso's hut, thus fueling his hatred for Ngo. Bender liked the rival chiefs equally well. Priso often visited Bender in the evenings, smoking his pipe and playing the Ndinga (a kind of zither) and singing songs, but he had in fact little administrative ability. Ngo was a less attractive personality, but he had the qualities of chieftancy, though he was somewhat of a conniver. Bender prepared a European feast of bowls of fish, potatoes, and palm oil sauce, and invited both leaders independently.

Priso arrived first, dressed in a colorful loin cloth, his upper body visibly scarred by earlier battles. Bender seated him alongside a box of choice tobacco far superior to the weeds that the natives puffed. Priso was soon engulfed in a cloud of smoke. Then, garbed in a white European suit, came Ngo, greeting Bender with a respectful bow. Priso shifted like an infuriated lion about to pounce upon its prey, yet was riveted and speechless. The two leaders spoke not a word. As soon as Ngo seated himself Bender pushed the tobacco box toward him, even as the cook was bringing in huge freshly baked breads and containers of steaming food. Bender sat between his two guests. Priso had a harder time manipulating European eating utensils than did Ngo but after finishing the obviously relished meal they both lit their pipes and relaxed. Watching covertly from concealed vantage points, occupants of the nearby mission house were amazed at the apparent reconciliation when the erstwhile rivals began acting civilly toward each other and, on finishing their smoke, thanked Bender for the occasion and left in seeming harmony.

If local food and the conditions for enjoying it with the natives at first tested Bender's missionary dedication, no less did overnight lodgings sometimes required during his three-week travel circuit and other trips. To be sure, in villages where natives had in the recent past made Christian commitments, there was everywhere a welcome. Yet there were inconveniences aplenty when, with little more than his walking stick, he set off now and then on an extended journey. Confronted unexpectedly once by a water buffalo and once by a crocodile he soon learned that water buffalo, like elephants, are relatively harmless if not provoked. But at one of the outstations he helped destroy a fifteen-foot snake that was devouring a small antelope—

skin, hair, and bones. Whatever the other deficiencies, if any, in his seminary preparation, he had not learned about snake-killing, nor had he learned to swim, a fact which left divine providence his only help when flimsy canoes maneuvered dangerous creeks and rivers. On one occasion when his overloaded canoe capsized, Bender escaped drowning by grasping an overhanging tree branch; on another, when he lost his balance and fell backward into the river, native helpers rescued him legs first.

Once after a hard day-long trek, Bender and his aides sought shelter in a seemingly deserted village. All at once a group of hunters armed with spears appeared from nowhere and just as suddenly disappeared back into the jungle. Bender encouraged his aides to shout: "A man of God has come! Hear what he has to say about God!" These hunters had never seen a white man, and like many others believed that the devil is white. Gradually they reemerged and while his aides sat on the ground nearby Bender spoke to the hunters of the love of God.

The variety of experiences in overnight lodgings were far different from what any tour agency could possibly offer. Once, en route to Buea, Bender slept in a native hut on the only available bed. Fortunately it was raised above ground, and therefore could harbor two squealing pigs beneath him, rats scurrying about, while on the rafters above him roosted several cackling chickens. It was a night either to forget or to remember. On another trip Bender wrapped himself in blankets and slept until about midnight when an itching, burning sensation roused him. The whole area and he in it were covered by crawling big black ants. He promptly joined his happy aides outside roasting potatoes around a fire. Bender soon learned how and when to use torches against such attacks.

In 1901 an epidemic of chicken pox swept Aboland

and many natives died. One slave village was noticeably spared, a deliverance that inhabitants attributed to protection by the village fetish. They accordingly brought and sacrificed many goats, sheep, and other items at the shrine of the fetish. To the natives' astonishment, however, the fetish priest himself then fell victim to the disease.

Bender often had to cope with superstitions related to fetishes. At stake was not merely a war of words but a conflict of powers. Trust in fetishes was best shattered when claims for the living God were accompanied by the unexpected nonfulfillment of superstitious expectations. Totemism likewise was rampant. On one occasion a herd of swine had greatly damaged a potato patch, but villagers were forbidden to interfere. The swine, they believed, were allegedly possessed by the spirits of Bakwiri women who would die if the swine were injured.

While the early human context for Bender's mission was largely squalor, superstition, and ignorance, its redeeming overruling text remained always the Bible, with its declared saving grace of God. He learned quickly, however, that a missionary cannot concentrate on preaching to the neglect of numerous other tasks. The agenda continually included counseling, advising chiefs, making peace amid squabbles, and an assortment of medical helps, such as applying hot plasters. Bender's home made laxative—a mixture cooked of castor oil, black coffee, fish oil, pepper, and sugar—became so famous that a native once came with six empty beer cans to be filled to the top.

Bender concluded early on that seminary rules of homiletics may at times need to suffer violence in a pioneer ministry to natives. Preaching had to be very simple and more in the nature of a conversation rather than the elaboration of a given text. He used both nature and social custom or practice as a point of contact. Sunday school classes were where he expounded Scripture and encouraged systematic Bible study. Since natives viewed tradition as sacred it was imperative to correct error tactfully. Love and patience were prerequisite to future harvest. Despite their superstitions about the spirit world, the natives were materialistic and concentrated on the here-and-now; "rice Christians" could easily emerge if the missionary's message neglected its spiritual priorities.

As did most other missionaries who trudged through mosquito-infested swamps, Bender came down frequently with malaria and several times with black water fever during his initial term.

In 1902 Bender went to Duala to welcome on arrival Valentin Wolff, one of his seminary companions. Wolff had joined Bender in Bonakwase for only a few days when he was smitten with malaria. Bender nursed him to recovery, only himself to fall victim to the disease later in the month. If one keeps in mind Bender's unique treatment of Wolff's affliction, this turn of things may seem like deserved retribution, but Wolff in fact later appropriated and improved on Bender's recovery process.

When Wolff began shivering, turned alternately hot and cold, complained of a headache and of leg and arm pains, he was put to bed without clothes, covered with a stack of blankets, and given hot tea and hot lemonade. When the patient began to perspire a half-hour later, more blankets were added for an additional two-hour confinement. Then Wolff was told to get up for a sponge bath on the porch of the hut. There Bender took a pail of fresh cold water and drenched the naked patient. Wolff had to admit that he had both survived and improved, and that the treatment had "worked." Wolff then manufactured a "sweat box" that provided more elegant service. He produced steam heat in a bed-covering canopy that virtually broiled the patient, and a less dramatic way of administering cold water. Wolff's sweat box became a routine means of malaria treatment at Kamerun mission stations.

When the first furlough drew near in 1903, Bender sailed from Duala with the exhortation of missionary colleagues that he return with a wife. She could, they suggested, in his visitation absences protect his hut against marauding mice and rats, and perhaps teach him more civilized methods of healing the sick.

Because of the rigorous responsibility assigned him to missionize twenty small relatively unreached villages beyond Duala, Bender often felt overwhelmed and even lonely. His colleagues' parting admonitions and his own growing thoughts of having a mission-minded wife as a co-worker and loving life companion deepened throughout the 1903 furlough in Germany.

Arrival and developments at Baptist Mission headquarters near Berlin soon helped solve Bender's needs and queries. Employed there as hostess and general household helper was Hedwig Kloeber who from various furloughing missionaries had heard interesting tales about hard-working but somewhat eccentric, often unshaven, and barefoot-wandering Carl Bender. Now in 1903 she met him face to face. The carefully prepared lunch she promptly served him was just as promptly but politely refused; four years in early Kamerun without dental care was the reason. For all that, Bender seemed pleasant and a gentleman as he discussed Kamerun affairs with Mission Director Mascher (successor to the retired Scheve), and as he greeted her during his comings and goings.

Born and reared near Dresden as a strict but somber state-Lutheran, Hedwig during a walk one day politely accepted a religious tract from a pleasant lady who invited her to a ladies' meeting at a nearby church. Impressed by the woman's sincerity and joyful demeanor, Hedwig went that very night to a small Baptist chapel. The spirit of personally experienced Christ-relatedness was so compelling there that Hedwig returned time and again for teaching, preaching, and fellowship. Soon, converted herself, she sealed her confession of faith with believer's immersion baptism, and became a Baptist. She became, in fact, the first Baptist in her hometown village. She was the only one of forty persons who accepted a proffered tract from the Baptist lady on that, for Hedwig, God-ordained day.

When she and Bender met in 1903 Hedwig was a pretty, smiling, brown-eyed, brown-haired Saxon lass of twenty-two. Already trained by then as a deaconess with qualifications and experience in practical nursing, biblical knowledge, social work, and visitation, she had secretly prayed about joining the growing number of appointees to Kamerun. Her additional ministry as helper and hostess at the Baptist headquarters reenforced her readiness and maturity for overseas work.

One morning Hedwig found a note tucked under her bedroom door. Dated Septermber 21, 1903, it read:

"Miss Hedwig Kloeber:

"Revered Sister!

"Pardon me that I approach you so unexpectedly
with a question whose answer is of great
significance not only for me personally, but also
for the work of the mission. The question is this--
could you decide to become my life companion
and to share with me the work in Kamerun?

"For a long time I have admired your quiet
manner, your piety, and the propriety of your
entire life, and, may I add, I love you from
my heart, and desire you above all others for
my wife. Decide with God. May I perchance
await an answer in the course of this week?

In joyful hope,
Carl J. Bender"

How and when Hedwig responded affirmatively to
this proposal is not recorded. In any case the couple's
wedding ceremony, conducted by Mission Director
Mascher in the German Baptist Mission headquarters, took
place on May 7, 1904. After a short visit with Hedwig's
relatives, Carl and Hedwig Bender made a memorable trip
to the United States. It was Bender's first return to his
Buffalo, New York, home and family since his 1899
farewells. Also significant was Hedwig's first meeting with
her new American relatives. For several crowded weeks
the happy couple visited Kamerun-supporting churches
and sampled denominational regional conferences.
Returning to Germany they promptly transferred to
Africa-bound transport.

On board ship Bender taught Hedwig basic Duala
words and phrases to ease her immediate assumption of
Duala duties and relationships. Both blacks and whites
were on hand to welcome the return of Bender and to
witness especially the arrival of his fortunately well-chosen
wife. She in fact was no total stranger to some of the
greeters, for she had met and helped various furloughed
workers at the German Mission Center.

Full staff resumptions of school and training
responsibilities, church growth involvements, evangelistic
trips and outreach, health services, and essential food
production were soon again underway in the expanding

Duala country. Between 1904 and 1908 the Benders would both assume increased leadership in Duala and contemplate a requested 1909 transfer to Soppo.

"To Bender the Bible was the supreme book of life, God's inerrant Word disclosing Christ's unique redemption available to all mankind. He studied it systematically every morning, taking from it for each day some specially pertinent admonition or promise."

5
BERLIN-SCHEVE

Until 1898, a year before Bender's departure for Africa, Eduard Scheve of the Hamburg-Oncken connection, almost one-handedly held the leadership fort, so to speak, for German Baptist interest in Kamerun. With the pastor's blessing he, with 200 members of a well-established church in old West Berlin, left to organize a church in newly settled East Berlin.

There, on Sunday, August 4, 1889, Alfred Bell, nephew of Kamerun's King Bell, dropped in to attend services. He had read the church's ad in a local newspaper (*Berliner Zeitung*, established 1877). Perhaps because of home recollections, not to mention divine prompting, he stepped that day into what became more than a church building. He accepted a proffered relationship of eternal significance for himself and for, in time, multitudes of Kamerunians.

Pastor Scheve's prompt hospitality and interest turned the key to multiple mission opportunities thousands of miles away. His continuing personal relationship with Bell planted a seed, moreover, that, however slow-growing, helped produce concepts of present-day missiology such as racial equality, economic and administrative cooperation, and leadership formulation.

Kamerun officials, as Scheve learned, had sent Bell to Europe on business where two years of homeless wandering in Western cultural wildernesses had done havoc to his earlier Christian instruction and commitment. Here in Berlin, however, Scheve's shepherding and his church's welcoming outreach climaxed on November 2, 1889, in Bell's and five other believers' public confession of faith and baptism. About 1200 persons witnessed and celebrated the occasion.

Among other things that Bell shared with Scheve was news of rampant confusion among native Baptists in Kamerun. Two groups—one, of self-directed independents who had seceded from imposed Basel control, and another group established and supervised by early white missionaries—vacillated back and forth on matters of cooperation and control. The independents had developed more and larger churches and trained leaders than had the more recently arrived but pressuring white missionaries. The independents called for help and perhaps mediation.

Scheve at once wrote to the London Baptist Mission Society, Basel Mission, and other reputable sources for their comments and evaluations. With about forty replies in hand, including one from Kamerun Governor von Soden, Scheve contacted Alfred Bell's church in Akwa. There were Baptists in Germany, he said, who wished to extend their hand of brotherhood to the Kamerunians. Highly respected Pastor Wilson answered at once: "The words of your letter—'be assured, dear brother, that warm hearts beat for you in Germany'—roused a storm of joy in the hearts of church members; everyone was moved and several wept. My old mother to whom I read the letter ... practically collapsed and cried with joy. I thought she'd never stop. Finally she said, 'Yes, if God be for us who can be against us?'"

The year 1891 finally brought long hoped-for interest by the Hamburg-Oncken enclave for supporting Kamerun missions and establishing an authentic German Baptist Missionary Society. Still in operation, however, was Scheve's personally instituted Mission Fellowship group that with him as director had overseen the sending and support of the earliest white missionaries. Conviction and pressure grew, however, to replace this Fellowship with a state incorporated organization. On November 28, 1898, the Kaiser legally incorporated just such an institution. The insights and practical helps that Scheve gained at Barmen conferences under Gustav Warneck (1834–1910), Germany's leading missiologist, played a part in this move.

Among new procedures would be democratic election of various duty-defined officers to replace appointments by any one person (Scheve was graciously elected as the first director, however). Membership would be international, moreover, a reflection perhaps of Oncken's early and now flourishing Baptist work throughout continental Europe and elsewhere. Both Baptists and non-Baptists from Austria, Russia, Holland, Switzerland, America, Australia, and India, for example, accordingly became members of this new society, a fact that in later pre- and post-War history would envision hopes for world, not regional, thinking.

This new Berlin organization appointed and supported both American German Baptists, Bender among them, as well as Europeans. Although North Americans contributed financially to the work at first, the realities of World War I necessarily cancelled such participation. In time the German Americans therefore founded their own foreign mission society to take over orphaned ministries and workers like the Benders and to enlist appointees of their own. While such organizational transitions posed work and personnel problems in both Germany and America, they eventually also clarified and encouraged mission procedures.

After Alfred Bell's stay in Germany, Eduard Scheve and his family for nine years hosted Kamerunians in their home, six altogether including two girls; some of them stayed for as long as six years. These guests shared bedrooms with the Scheve children, attended the same schools, and enjoyed the same activities and associations as their German sponsors. Among these extended family participants was Richard Edube Mbene, who as a result became the first specially prepared native to teach seminarians in both Duala and Soppo. He and Bender partnered well in leadership training.

As for Alfred Bell, he was among the first persons to greet August Steffens and his wife in 1891 on their arrival in Victoria from the United States. It was he, moreover, who persuaded Steffens to leave Victoria and to proceed to Dualaland. After all, it was King Bell's people and church members with whom Scheve had originally clasped hands and hearts. As for Scheve, the long, patience-taxing struggle begun in early Hamburg days and continued in Berlin for a functioning, independent, and incorporated German Baptist Mission Society was now triumphantly over.

6

BUEA

Berlin-appointed governors—knowingly or not and for better or worse—determined many situations in Kamerun. The six in office during that colony's existence were the following:

Julius von Soden (1885–1891)
Eugen von Zimmerer (1891–1895)
Jesko von Puttkamer (1895–1907)
Dr. Theodor Seitz (1907–1910)
Dr. Otto Gleim (1910–1912)
Karl Ebermaier (1912–1915)

Bender as a missionary knew and functioned under the last four. (His additional post-World War I ministry occurred during the period of British and French mandates instituted by the League of Nations. He therefore served during three colonial administrations—German, British, and French.)

Of the above-named governors, Prussian Jesko von Puttkamer was perhaps the most entrepreneurially involved in Kamerun's development. Brother-in-law of Bismarck and close friend of Hamburg's merchant magnate Woermann, he was no stranger to political and international affairs. After stints as German Consul in British Lagos and German Togo, von Puttkamer became governor of the latter. From Togo he proceeded to Kamerun, first as chancellor, then as governor.

His Togo departure December 2, 1895, at three a.m., marked him as properly knowledgeable about tropical weather and temperature precautions. In any case at that pre-dawn hour, Kru boys (prized Liberian-born Pidgin-English speaking boatmen famous for outsmarting the Atlantic's unpredictable turbulence and for negotiating rock and sandbar hurdles) rowed him for two hours to an off-shore sea-going vessel. Although soaked and, as he reported, "filthy," he clambered up the customary overside rope ladder to board ship. Because of reputedly little fresh food in Kamerun, he took along forty-eight sheep, twelve of which drowned.

At his first stop Lagos he met Eduard Schmidt, an old friend; it was Schmidt who as merchant Woermann's agent had helped negotiate the Duala Kings' transfer of land to German Consul Nachtigal and then hoisted the German flag to confirm colonial occupation. Von Puttkamer socialized as well with British Sir Frederick Carter, his former political associate. Remembering Lagos only too well as a famous horse- breeding, horse-racing metropolis, he also bought two horses, notwithstanding Kamerun's animal-unfriendly tsetse fly problems. Together with sheep, horses, and carefully chosen, preferred Togo servants, von Puttkamer finally proceeded to Victoria.

Here yet another friend, Dr. Preusz, director of Kamerun's celebrated Botanical Garden, welcomed him, but with startling news: Bakwiri rebels had attacked Buea. The skirmish, moreover, had cost the life of revered explorer Graf von Gravenreuth. Things in Duala were not much better; British-oriented King Akwa still functioned boldly as ruler despite official transfer of his domain from English connections to German control. Stepping forward to advise von Puttkamer was yet another rediscovered friend, Richard Spengler. Having, said Spengler, himself quelled some of his own problems by developing plantations, perhaps von Puttkamer should do the same. Gaining Berlin's permission, von Puttkamer therefore sold friend Spengler 10,000 hectares of land around Mt. Cameroon. In so doing he collaborated in establishing West African Plantation Victoria that in time became one of the largest such operations in the world.

This commercial land appropriation or misappropriation initiated serious consequences for both the people and country of Kamerun. Already by the turn of the century 10,000 natives, sometimes unwillingly, were under contract as plantation workers to twenty-three different firms. Disruption of families, of clans and tribes, dissolution of entire villages through population shifts, disruption of schools and churches, degrading social situations—all followed in due course. While economic and commercial growth and development soared, they did so in many ways at the expense of human worth and dignity, and of proper government as well.

Jesko von Puttkamer encouraged and himself practiced vigorous criss-crossing of Kamerun. Besides establishing for immediate occupation geographically and commercially significant cities and stationing military garrisons throughout the colony, he also transferred the country's capitol in 1902 from steamy Duala to more salubrious Buea. He also drew and fixed the country's borders. Under his direction natives built roads and railroads and even discovered oil (lack of funds tabled this particular find for some time). At Buea, within walking distance of Soppo he built a palatial residence to ease his housing problems which to this day is still used. In earlier days merchants and even officials often replaced the sails or other topdeck gear of their sea-going vessels with simple poled structures roofed over with weather-resistant materials. These moveable hulks, as they were called, provided living accommodations and space for buying, selling, and general business affairs. Von Puttkamer never used his luxurious sea-going craft in this way but reserved it for frequent travel whenever and wherever he chose. His Buea palace became the nation's official residence.

Politically astute and industriously creative, von Puttkamer's interests were largely commercial and secular. As already indicated, he was socially and internationally well-connected, and also known as an avid patron of the arts, especially of classical music, with which he surrounded himself. In the course of his operations and lifestyle he became equally known, however, for his reprehensible treatment of blacks and for his in-mansion philandering. Of necessity Berlin officials therefore recalled him in 1907, thereafter assigning governors more attuned to missions and missionaries' purposes and diligent in protecting Kamerunians' human and civil rights.

Bender's first two terms were under von Puttkamer's jurisdiction. His very name must at times have brought to mind Jesko's relative, Alexander von Puttkamer, who in America had founded and pastored Bender's home church in Buffalo, New York, and as evangelist, preacher, and overall religious leader had strengthened both German and American Baptist development.

In 1908 Governor Dr. Theodor Seitz replaced von Puttkamer. Buea rather than Duala was still the colony's capitol; plantation operations had engulfed more and more territory and more and more workers. Growth of mission work and mission personnel followed in due course.

German Mission Director Mascher's 1908 official Kamerun visit was timely.

On arrival in Victoria, instead of taking the new narrow-gauge plantation trolley to Soppo and Buea, Mascher chose to walk there by moonlight from 10:30 p.m. to 4:00 a.m. the next day. Doing so replicated at least something of what early, often work-worn and sickly missionaries did regularly. His joy at being welcomed by friends would surely match that of early personnel who at journey's end embraced waiting loved ones and co-workers. Mascher's also latching on to a missionary readying himself for a two-week stint of bush village visitation exposed him to yet another important phase of missionary work. Significant as well was Mascher's requested conference with the new mission-friendly governor. Their two-hour cordial visit manifested Seitz's sincere personal and official appreciation of the presence and influence of missions and missionaries in general and of the Baptist work in particular. To help strengthen inter-mission relationships Mascher also apprized himself about Basel ministries and workers. His reports of such on-site experiences would surely heighten missions comprehension and support.

Two years later in 1910 Karl Mascher's attendance at the historic Edinburgh Mission Conference exposed him to international and interdenominational mission percepts and precepts. It would also stretch his access to fellowship with other Great Commission proponents. Among them was John Mott, whose well-received worldwide mission experience and influence would in time help formulate the World Council of Churches and its operations. In any case the Edinburgh challenge for inter-mission concerns and relationships would in time echo its way to Kamerun.

For Bender, Buea was much closer than many of his

outlying villages and substations. The new capitol city's location only a half-hour's walk from Soppo therefore made it a frequent port of call for him. As missions', missionaries', churches', and schools' importance and authenticity grew in colonial affairs, government officials and others relocated from Duala found the Benders' nearby compound similarly advantageous for them.

Troublesome encounters with rebel Buea Bakwiris had been largely settled by the time of the Benders' move to Soppo, and Buea was no longer just a cluster of deserted Bakwiri huts of earlier times. Disappearing, if not already gone, were the narrow interlocking mountain paths between traders' villages and markets. Now a broad road past lovely landscaping, European homes, business installations and well-kept Bakwiri quarters were a far cry from deliberately secluded retreats of tribesmen porters who plied their wares to waiting overlords. What now replaced slaves as the major item of international trade was ivory, especially the flawless tusks of Mt. Cameroon elephants. Altogether Kamerun in 1893 alone had exported over 65,000 kilograms of ivory worth 755,000 German marks at a slaughter-cost of about 940 elephants. The Boanda market beyond Buea would be long remembered for the best ivory in all of West Africa.

While on some exploratory and missions-extending trips Bender carried a gun against surprise encounters, his journeys up the slopes of Mt. Cameroon would not ordinarily have required such caution. Of greater concern to him than wild animals was the Bakwiris' ongoing fear of the mountain's reported evil spirits.

Soon after Soppo arrival he therefore climbed a good part of volcanic Mt. Cameroon beyond Buea to help disprove the existence of death-dealing beings or forces. Were the mountain's occasional eruptions—that of 1905 had been the most recent—responsible for their fear? At such quakes, according to oral tradition, tongues of fire became white wraiths that floated up and around the mountain.

There had been previous climbers, of course, often doing scientific research. Although related in part to some of his personal interests, Bender's real climbing motivation was nonetheless unique in being perhaps the first known effort to help eradicate the Bakwiris' dread of and submission to Mt. Cameroon's lurking spirit powers. Involved for Bender as well in this climb was suppression of local or itinerant magicians whose self-touted trickery promised gullible villagers protection from evil spirits— for a price, of course.

Because the seemingly embodied mountain spirits were both evil and white, many tribal chiefs identified them as of the devil. During Bender's earliest years in Duala's out-lying substations, people, when he first arrived, ran away into nearby jungles because he was white and therefore must be the devil. Now in the extended Soppo-Buea area the problem for many Bakwiris was not identifying him as the white devil but rather fearing often fog-shrouded, presumably spirit-inhabited Mt. Cameroon as a place of no return.

Would Bender return from his climb or become a victim of evil spirits? Bender's safe return from this first ascent (with two but carefully secreted skulls) definitely helped discount, even eradicate some of the Bakwiris' long-held traditions. In time more and more Europeans and also natives scaled the Mighty Mountain. Some blacks, in fact, eventually sponsored competitive marathons up and down its challenging slopes.

Bender Memorial Church set against Mt. Cameroon
His last major project (building) in Soppo

7
SOPPO 1

No matter how long one lives in a foreign country or even in one's own, omniscience about its history and people is quite unlikely. Even mature missionaries know that their varied daily ministries often uncover new facts and insights. In this sense the Benders' initial terms in extended Duala stood them in good stead for knowing not only the Dualas but also the Bakwiris (also called Wakwelis) and other tribes. Their assignment in 1909 was to Soppo, to develop the small Baptist church and school ministries and to manage the missionaries' Rest and Recovery Center. When tropical or other illnesses invaded missionaries' lives it was becoming financially prohibitive and moreover too unsettling to mission work continuity simply to go on home leave.

Already in 1899 Duala-based Missionary Tromsdorf had gone to Soppo and erected a temporary sheet metal structure of two assembly rooms and a small housing area. Serious Aboland problems required an early return to Duala, however. Missionary Hofmeister then took over the Soppo project and completed the masonry work. His stay was shortlived as well when serious illness furloughed him to Germany.

Meanwhile, wood and cement specially gathered in

Hamburg for Soppo construction had arrived in Victoria. There it lay, however, at Pastor Wilson's home for one-and-a-half years, canopied but nonetheless subject to termites and tropical weathering. Lack of human porters was the problem. Next in line to arrive in Soppo to tackle and hopefully solve the long-delayed building problem were Missionaries Nissen and Schwarz. Confronting them in 1902, first of all, was the still unsolved matter of needed porters. (Not until four years later would the Victoria Plantation Company have its narrow-gauge railroad in place. What's more, Bakwiri men were happily under contract to well-paying government and plantation employers). All requests and searches for human transport seemed futile. Was there any hope at all for completing the Soppo Mission and Rest Center before the May-June rainy season?

Just when human helplessness reached its worst, God again manifested himself as the Supreme Implementor of his Kingdom work. He ordained it that a Duala Christian, then residing in Buea near Soppo, gained listening access to Governor von Puttkamer. In short order 150 prisoners released to do four Soppo-to-Victoria porterage trips for the Governor were assigned by him to add a fifth such seven-hour, twenty-two-mile trip, this time in reverse from Victoria-to-Soppo and for the Baptist Mission.

With the Victoria load of building supplies now moved, the next problem for Missionaries Nissen and Schwarz was securing carpenters. This time a teacher leaving Soppo for Duala became God's helper. (Telephone service was still two years off.) Apprized by the returning teacher of Soppo's plight, Duala Missionary and Director Suevern in short order sent eight such workmen. By the end of May 1903, the Soppo project was finished.

All that remained to do now was to replace temporary

supports with a ten-centimeter square concrete pillar to bear the weight of the building. With this task accomplished there was certainly now good reason to celebrate. No festive singing, no speeches hailed this climax, however. No spectators were present. Only a few native laborers and two missionaries joined hearts and hands in a gesture of dedication. Into a large bottle they quietly placed a written thanksgiving to God, a record of the building's construction process, names of the participating laborers and missionaries, a few coins and stamps, and several current periodicals. With a sense of God's "Well done" they buried this treasure in the plinth of the pillar, there to await some future historian's discovery and amazement, or perchance—as the world turns—even some catastrophe or willful destruction.

The first official occupants of the Soppo house—it was they who witnessed the final aspect of construction and carried out the unique dedication—were Missionary and Mrs. W. Märtens. In a thank you letter of appreciation to ladies in Germany Frida Märtens acknowledged receipt of curtains for the health center and listed the need of extra bed linens, towels, tablecloths, and draperies to augment her present supplies. Desired most of all, however, she underscored the always requisite gift of faithful prayer. "Our lovely large house," she wrote, "is 750 meters up the Mt. Kamerun slopes and within easy access to both government offices and Governor von Puttkamer's mansion. At present we have seven rooms—three occupied by us, three available for recuperating guests, and one for general fellowship. In the last-named we spend many happy hours, almost forgetting being in reputedly deadly Africa. We were recently reminded of this unhappy characterization, however, when we learned that Mrs. Reimer, who just a few months ago had recovered so well among us, had died. Most of our guests, in fact, usually arrive very ill and exhausted, longing for the rest of mind and body that our Soppo program offers."

Her letter continued:

"Mornings at six o'clock the school bell summons students and villagers for united worship and rouses house guests from their beds. All meals, including seven o'clock breakfast, are served in the house-encircling veranda. During early conversations it's not unusual to hear, 'It's terribly cold here!' or even 'I'm freezing!' Night temperatures at Soppo sometimes drop to 10 degrees. Scarves, sweaters, and hot food come to the rescue.

"Devotions and singing led by various people follow in the living room. Personal pursuits and refreshing garden walks then fill the guests' remaining morning hours.

"Meantime, school is underway, often with the male missionary in charge. At the same time his wife treats assembled patients and dispenses medicines before defining and supervising helpers' duties in the kitchen.

"Following a light noon lunch comes enforced siesta until two o'clock to avoid outside exposure to the hottest, most debilitating, and even dangerous period of the day. Outdoor activity and recreation for guests soon returns thereafter, however, while native women and their daughters gather for missionary instruction in sewing and household management. At four o'clock dismissed school girls come for an hour of handcraft lessons.

"At five o'clock we do village visitation to help families and individuals with personal and community problems.

"Dinner at 6:30 followed by evening devotions and leisurely review of the day's experiences ready all of us for recuperative sleep and commitment to God's care.

"Obviously such heavy and structured missionary schedules are subject to change because of unforeseen interruptions such as illness. Being always available to our house guests if at all possible, is essential, of course. Every effort is made to help renew exhausted workers for happy and effective resumption of their ministries."

Such delineation by Frida Märtens of life at Soppo informed interested supporters in Germany and provided a helpful model for successor directors-to-be like the Benders.

The register of pioneer missionaries to venture Soppo and other construction projects had been amazing. Though generally in good health, several within a short time were forced to withdraw from such work. Notwithstanding, even they together with their hardier co-workers left more than mere thumb prints in the miscellaneous early hammering and cementing of mission expansion.

Bender Conducting Baptisms

8
SOPPO 2
(Bender–1909)

The Benders' relocation to Soppo in 1909 remained a welcome challenge. Stretching upward almost within stone's throw was Mt. Cameroon, "Mountain of God," as the natives called it. Victoria and Duala were within solid trekking distance; less than an hour's walk away was the capitol city Buea. The area's usually temperate climate was the kind that Bender would surely have welcomed during his earlier malaria and black water fever attacks in Duala. Even at more healthful Soppo, however, being outside between 10:30 a.m. and 2 p.m. during November to February was discouraged; temperatures could soar to 102 degrees.

The Benders remembered only too well their and others' earlier climbs on stony, rough roads to visit Soppo. During the last hour or so of such trips women sometimes had to be carried on "hammocks," canvas sheets strapped to a crossbar. Now as a part of their own Rest Center hostessing program the Benders therefore determined to meet arriving guests at least an hour's distance from Soppo, bringing them refreshing lunch and relieving them of luggage.

Tackling the mission site's unkempt acreage was another of Bender's early Soppo decisions. With hard work and help from black seminarians whose leadership training could benefit from knowing something about property development and maintenance, he created a veritable Eden.

For his garden framework he assembled towering palms and low-growing bushes. Inside this border he placed fruit-bearing mango trees and a crescent-shaped, ivy-covered rock garden. Elsewhere a fountain splashed heavenward from a sparkling pool. Nearby stretched croquet-ready turf. In quiet nooks of this paradisiacal garden Bender tucked personally fashioned benches, tables, and chairs. Coordinating these health-quickening arrangements were safety-assuring flagstone pathways.

Within view of the Rest Center at a height of 2500 feet Bender and his team raised bananas, plantains, oranges, limes, grapefruit, avocadoes, Batanga cherries, guavas, pomegranates, papaya, pineapples , and grapes. He raised coffee and tea. Closer at hand was his vegetable garden. Bountiful fruits and vegetables together with dairy products for Benders' patients constituted daily menus.

Across the years not only would Rest Center patrons and the Baptist mission use and appreciate this extraordinary compound, but also World War I invaders and beyond that, generations-to-come of colonially freed, self-governing Cameroonians.

Because of marauding animals, Bender fenced in his vegetable garden. One rumor, usually reported with a wink, portrayed him as on one occasion capturing an intruding goat. Lacing its horns with burning dry grass he promptly rocketed the poor creature into the wilds. It bothered Bender that natives allowed livestock to wander through his precious garden. Even though perhaps converted, these people seemed to find no connection between salvation and proper control of their animals!

The Soppo Rest Center building was surrounded on all sides by a roofed veranda. Here meals were served, various conferences took place, and all visitors were entertained. Inside rooms were reserved for office work and for sleeping. The Benders' schedule much like the Märtens' was well-ordered. At six all Kamerunians came to morning worship at the combined school and chapel building. Women carrying waterpots from the village for later filling usually arrived early. Missionaries and other Europeans gathered at the Rest Center for their own time of prayer before dispersing to various pursuits. Before school began at eight o'clock Hedwig Bender treated children for skin diseases or other ailments. The next hour she spent with adults to treat toothaches, wounds aggravated by sand fleas or termites, and to dole out castor oil, especially enjoyed and requested by the natives. Then came household orientation to helpers. Thereafter she visited people in their huts, bringing physical and spiritual help as needed. In later years Britain granted her a certificate of recognition for her work.

After noon lunch, sometimes consisting of African fare of potatoes, oil, dried fish, and pepper, compulsory rest prevailed until 1:30. Then, until late afternoon came sewing classes interspersed with hymn sings and Bible lessons for as many as thirty girls. Servants shared in after-supper devotions. Only thereafter the Benders took their daily walk to enjoy the flowers and to plan the next day's activities.

During full moon things were a bit different. Missionaries wore straw helmets outside to protect against moonstroke; so bright was the moon that one could almost read without extra light. Indoor lamplighting at 7:30

brought opportunities for fellowship and perhaps for handling correspondence.

Like Hedwig, Carl Bender also maintained a given schedule. After early supervision of the school, he returned home at nine o'clock for his favorite snack, a roasted African sweet potato. From time to time his activities included road-building, laying water pipes, painting, and mending or replacing roofs, tasks for which he used his trained native helpers. (During one of Hedwig's infrequent absences he painted all the veranda's rattan furniture a flaming red.) Like Mrs. Bender, he, too, visited natives in their huts, prepared there to meet any number of situations.

Religious services included Wednesday night prayer meetings alongside intensive Bible study, supplemented by the reading of Bender's helpful Bakwiri or Duala notes. For regularly scheduled often week-long teachers' gatherings Bender shaped study and discussion materials. Sunday was always the crowning day of the week, however. Sunday school from nine to ten, in English, Duala, and German was followed from ten to eleven by a church worship service. Sunday afternoons the Benders ministered regularly at both the government prison and nearby plantations.

Arranging and implementing entire Soppo district conferences for about 400 Christians, some of whom walked twenty or more miles to participate, was another of Bender's major responsibilities.

Not to be forgotten, moreover, were his trips, often lasting three weeks, to visit every outlying station. His favorite Bible verse on such travels was Exodus 33:14, "My presence goeth before thee." Supplementing this promise was his favorite hymn, "Sinners Jesus Will Receive," which he often sang out loud to himself or asked native helpers to sing along with him.

Bender enjoyed walking, often with God and his thoughts as his only companions. Always with cane in hand, he walked with head erect, sometimes stumbling into people. If they joshed him for being aloof or snobbish, he explained he was mentally at work on a sermon. Of the several walking sticks he had carved from coffee, tea, and palm wood his favorite was a knotty one with an iron claw base like those preferred by Alpine climbers. Such a model had many uses on longer journeys.

Sometimes Bender did what was then considered unthinkable, and thereby endeared himself to the natives. Once when a torrential rain overtook him and his native helper, Bender invited the aide to share not only his hut but also his bed for the night. Later on the same journey, this time parched by the hot sun, Bender asked a European for a bit of roadside rest in his shady compound. When the owner acquiesced, but stipulated that the native must remain outside, Bender declined such preferential hospitality, and with his helper continued hiking.

On longer trips Bender often used young blacks who earned their school tuition by helping him. Others covered school costs by working on the mission compound. In due course many such helpers became teachers or evangelists. After their six years of basic instruction those who seemed qualified added two more years in a government normal school. Such preparation usually readied them for both government and mission teaching.

During seminary days Bender was never considered a powerful speaker. One of his professors, aware that Bender's writing propensity exceeded that of preaching proficiency, observed that his student's marriage of poetry and theology was strange indeed. For all that, Bender did indeed preach effectively, not only in English but also in German and Duala; his trilingual writing of books and teaching-preaching   materials soon erased apprehensions about his communication skills. The expression of theology in   poetic   form,   moreover,   was   not   biblically unprecedented.

To Bender the Bible was the supreme Book of Life, God's   inerrant   Word   disclosing   Christ's   unique redemption available to all mankind. He studied it systematically every morning, taking from it for each day some specially pertinent admonition or promise.

While he himself never played a musical instrument, Bender thoroughly enjoyed others' renditions, especially on the violin. He sang a good baritone, but seldom soloed except on trips. Hedwig, on the other hand, sang both alto and soprano, and usually joined choirs wherever they lived.   Bender's   musical   contribution   lay   rather   in translating at least twenty-five hymns and gospel songs into Duala, some from German and others from English. He also composed hymns of his own which the natives learned   and   enjoyed.   Already   in   seminary   he   had partnered with his   friend   Grimmel   who   composed melodies to which Bender then supplied words.

Bender's clothing seemed a bit flamboyant, but not to the natives. He liked flashy red and green ties, for example, a predisposition that neither time nor family could remedy. In Africa he usually covered his bald head with a cork helmet. Very seldom available but especially treasured for its warmth during chilly Cameroon weather was a white Palm Beach suit. For gardening he wore khaki, and   early   on   had   wandered   shoeless   until   Hedwig stipulated a change. He reverted to shoelessness by necessity, however, when in the absence of African shoemakers, his overly-patched footgear became more uncomfortable and less acceptable than going barefoot.

Bender was not a pioneer in the usual sense of personally founding the Soppo—let alone Duala and Victoria—mission work. The term for him applied rather to his modeling and sharing with native co-workers and Western successors creative ways of daily thinking and of practicing biblically based principles of human dignity, vocational responsibility, and sociological accountability. Challenges of tribal, racial, and family relationships, legal and government responsibilities, work habits, business procedures, school, church, and community affiliations—in other words, comprehensive moral integrity—were Bender's passion.

German Baptists were not the first to envision Soppo as a possible mission site. Even before Germany's 1884 takeover of Dualaland, Basel Mission of Switzerland had established itself in various locations. In due course it sought access also to the Buea area and sent catechist Duala Johnson to visit the people of Soppo. His efforts in that regard were unsuccessful, however, because of the villagers' geographically extensive and scattered locations. When the natives reported this disappointment to Soppo Chief Sako, he appealed to his friend Pastor Wilson in Victoria for a permanent on-site church worker. Joseph Burnley, recently returned from ministerial training in Bristol, England, became that appointee.

Accompanied by several young men Burnley set about establishing the first mission building and shepherding a small group of converts. In other words, this beginning was entirely by natives. No white missionary was on hand until Reverend Schwarz arrived from Duala. Impressed by the Chief's and Pastor Burnley's promising Soppo involvement Schwarz happily joined the duo in their efforts. He and his wife, in fact, became one of the first temporary trial occupants of the early missionary quarters. When Wilson's death required Burnley's return to Victoria, Soppo became perceived as a basically stable and authentic mission station.

In 1909 when the Benders arrived in Soppo they at once made comity arrangements with nearby Basel Mission workers whose efforts deliberately concentrated on larger cities like Buea. Bender therefore opted to respect their territory and instead visited, evangelized, and established outlying villages as substations to Soppo. His success in such endeavors was manifest, indeed, in eventually founding at least thirty such Soppo-related communities.

In launching out to yet unreached areas Bender established a visitation program easily learned and in time often followed by the students who accompanied him. The first task, assigned to an aide lest Bender's whiteness be perturbing in some way, involved finding and greeting the village chief. His coming having been explained as being friendly, Bender then offered to build a school in the village and to supply a teacher and a teacher's hut. News was given in the conversation about chiefs in other villages who had already accepted such offers and found them of great benefit. If the newly met chief seemed disinterested or even belligerent, Bender nonetheless shook hands and journeyed on. Some time later he returned, however, and this time not as a total stranger repeated his offer to the now hopefully less recalcitrant chief.

In this way chiefs and villagers came to know about missionaries and their work which, of course, moved beyond building schools and supplying teachers to placing pastors, establishing churches, and shepherding converts. Also in this way Bender's students gained courage and experience for demonstrating and sharing their own Christian faith. If, in fact, as one of his Rochester seminary teachers had said, Bender's strength was not in preaching per se, that same professor later portrayed him as a spiritually empowered discipler of leaders.

Bender's written record of thirty in-training teachers and evangelists who later ministered in Soppo's outstations or elsewhere confirm this discipling relationship. Each person's vitae included the usual information about date and place of birth, age, schools attended, date of baptism, church connection, and date of ordination if realized. Then, gained from Bender's personal relationship and ministry observation, followed a summary of the young man's character strengths and weaknesses, his work success, level of personal maturity and independence, and areas needing correction and counsel. The fact that most of these men were born and educated in Soppo (others came from elsewhere to study there) indicates a wholesome second-generation strength of the local church. That many of these Soppo sons became workers in their own church's substations is equally noteworthy. The fact, moreover, that many of them would still carry the responsibilities of teaching, preaching, and evangelizing during the absent-missionary post-world War I era would be specially heartening and would verify their solid training and readiness for eventual independence. One can hardly imagine Bender's great joy on his later return to Soppo in 1929 to indeed find some of "his boys" still faithfully at work.

Surely these now soon-to-be self-reliant workers would not in the future forget their treks with Bender. Some of the problems that they and he confronted together would be overcome little by little. Later when isolated from missionary help and relationships, Bender's "boys" in retrospect would certainly cherish more than ever the fearless, physically taxing endeavors they and Bender undertook in earlier years to reach and win distant villages for the cause of Christ. In remembrance some might even smile or chuckle, as they shared unique experiences with their perhaps disbelieving children.

One such memorable Bender trip to observe and participate in an outstation's Sunday services had followed an unusually busy week in Soppo. At day's end, as was his custom, bone-weary Bender bedded down in a hospitable native's hut. There he joined three Kamerunians in smoke-blackened, windowless quarters three meters long, two meters wide, and three-and-a-half meters high. Mosquitos buzzed around their ears, nearby sheep bleated annoyance at the rain, and someone in an adjoining hut was moaning.

A new day finally dawned, however, bringing with it further trekking and crossing of rain-swollen rivers. One river proved especially hazardous because of rushing waterfalls. Strong as they were, Bender's helpers had trouble getting themselves, let alone Bender, across the roaring stream. Had several other natives on the opposite shore not come to the rescue, disaster would surely have ensued. With Bender's boys pushing desperately from behind, and the others who had jumped into the raging waters grabbing his legs from the front, Bender was shoved and pulled to safety from the threatening waterfalls. It would have been quite a sight had there been time or inclination to watch.

Often the next stop after still more travel hazards was Victoria. Having withdrawn from Basel affiliation, the Baptist church there had both internal and external problems; it needed help both in loosing itself from post-Saker foreign control and in maneuvering the tensions of independency.

At Victoria Bender also took time to visit the cemetery

and its ever accumulating missionary graves. He paused as well at the memorial to Horton Johnson, the first convert at Alfred Saker's first sermon at Fernando Po. In pondering this black evangelist's subsequent years of Saker partnership and his membership in Saker's first Duala church of five persons, Bender could only implore God, as he often did, for many more such native workers. Throughout his mission experience Bender firmly believed that Africa must be brought to Christ through her own converted sons and daughters. Europeans (a general term for whites) could and should be primarily encouragers and helpers.

From Victoria, dead tired and soaked to the skin after heavy rains, Bender that day nevertheless kept trekking. A day's rainfall of thirty or more inches was not unusual. Finally having reached and ministered at his last projected village and being now homeward-bound, travel hardships and even terrors lost their edge for Bender. Refreshing preaching and communion services along the way always evidenced God's presence and blessing. However exhausted and weary, he therefore returned to Soppo joyful of heart to be Christ's co-laborer and to have promising loyal helpers. Across many years with no transport but sturdy legs and feet maintained by the Lord, but in obedience to God's *Go ye* command, Bender and his trainee fellows covered literally thousands of Kamerun miles.

Much closer at hand, of course, was the capital city Buea. His having spent two terms in earlier capital city Duala and its environs with responsibility for twenty-two substations had readied Bender for the Buea-Soppo-Victoria transfer. In both locales, moreover, relationships with government officials and with Basel Mission leaders, their congregations and stations were no mere coincidence.

As mission expansion and interrelationships grew as well as interaction with political changes and commercial development, the perception and performance of missionaries and Christians would require increased acceptance and authentication.

Soppo Sunday School

9

FURLOUGH THREE (1913–1914)

As the Benders' departure to Berlin mission headquarters and meetings there with Director Mascher approached they realized how strong their ties to Africa had become. No less strong, however, were the ties to Germany where children Herbert, Erica, and Thorwald had been left in 1908 with a childless missions-friendly pastor and his wife. Fearing that the trio might be separated to different families, they insisted on caring for all three and did so for four years. Other missionaries' children were similarly separated from their parents and entrusted to loving sponsors.

Early Kamerun conditions necessitated such family arrangements. Not yet in place were hospitals, schools, let alone home-schooling concepts. Tropical disease control was not yet fully understood or practiced. Death statistics from malaria, black water fever, and various endemic diseases were appalling. Between 1893 and 1898 six German Baptist missionaries had died in Kamerun; between 1901 and 1912, eight had died, making a total of fourteen deaths in nineteen years. Other workers had cut short their assignments and returned home because of ill health.

In God's good time he provided an answer to this family and Mission Society problem. In March, 1911, through the estate of businessman F. W. Bergemann, the Baptist Mission had bought over 12,000 square acres of land outside Berlin near the benefactor's burial site in Neuruppin. It was he who had also provided— anonymously—the Hamburg materials for building the Soppo mission and rest center. A devout believer but never a Baptist adherent, Bergemann had learned about Baptists through the witness of one of his employees, and had thereafter volunteered significant helps to the Baptist Mission. The acreage bought in 1911 for a combined missionary children's home and accommodations for furloughing parents became a capstone of his self-giving life. By June, 1912, an attractive building was dedicated and ready for occupancy.

The Benders' 1913 furlough in Germany therefore included a special even unique family reunion. They took with them two Soppo-born children, Carl Ronald (1910) and Armin Ndedi (meaning "grace" in Duala) (1912) to

The Bender Family
in Germany about 1912

join and make friends with other children in the Neuruppin quarters. Among those new "friends" would be their own siblings Herbert, Erica, and Thorwald, whom Carl and Armin had never met and who had never met them, and whom their "foster" parents had surrendered with full understanding but deep regret. (Letters especially between Thorwald ("adopted" when only nine months old) and his "adoptive mother" continued through World War II and culminated in a reunion visit in the United States).

Seeing the Benders' own five and other workers' children now resident in special accommodations was cause for thanksgiving. Saying goodbye, however, was nonetheless still difficult for everyone concerned. Tears are but a part and not necessarily the easiest part of missions-related farewells and heartaches. But once again God's care and timing would overshadow the Benders' return to Kamerun and their children's safe-keeping in Germany.

In furlough meetings with Mission Board officials and supporting churches they shared news about the projected 1914 interdenominational Kamerun mission conference. They pled for prayer and cooperative project support.

Statistics spoke for themselves about progress from early trial-and-error-prone procedures and even personnel to more recent result-validating operations. In 1913 Basel Mission students now numbered 17,833, Catholics claimed 12,461, American Presbyterians reported 9,213, and the German Baptists, 3,151. Founded in the low or mid-1800s, each group had grown under dedicated missionaries but also and significantly by using trained and responsible native leaders and co-workers.

By 1914 at least some missionaries could therefore anticipate allotting more time and energy to writing, and to translating Bibles and teaching materials even as they helped de-Westernize worship and church procedures to more culturally relevant forms. In but a short time transfer or return to African approaches and expressions of Christian faith would fall into happy place.

For all that, Bender also espied on the mission horizon a creeping resurgence of long-held ethnic, colonial, and international tensions. Shortly impacting on Kamerun's future might be implosions of centuries-old inter-tribal, inter-racial, and inter-colonial hatred and dissension. Greedy, commercial dispossession of native land, excessive taxation of labor-deprived people, forced re- and dis-location of natives to accommodate white-city planning, illegal or ill-advised currying by blacks of English or German political favors. How, when, and by whom would or could such a formidable, ever-rising ladder of discontent be toppled for Kamerun's rescue and renewal? How would missionaries like the Benders and their ministry comrades, black and white, meet the claims upon them for God's truth and justice?

In March, 1914, the Benders returned from furlough to Soppo. Awaiting them was prompt preparation for what would be the first of hopefully many biennial inter-fellowship mission conferences. In just three months the interdenominational gathering was underway.

Following is Bender's report to the German Baptist Mission Society in Berlin:

"On Sunday afternoon, July 5, 1914, at a pre-conference devotional hour Soppo Missionary Bender reminded attendees not only of the importance and extent of their task, but also of the greatness and power of their Lord. It was an encouraging and faith-building reminder that the Lord not only indicates his servants' responsibilities but also that in their efforts to implement these tasks he will be their all in all. It is he who calls, who sends, who opens doors, who determines goals, who gives the increase. He is the risen mighty Lord. All power is his. He gives courage and strength to overcome all difficulties and hindrances. His will and his will alone must be determinative for his people. These thoughts were ongoingly expressed in discussions that followed. A time of testimony and for prayer closed the meeting.

"As one or another recalled difficult times and, especially, the personal sacrifices of their labors, the promise of Matthew 19:29 became all the more precious: 'He who has left houses or brothers or sisters or wife or children or property for my name's sake will receive hundred-fold and inherit eternal life.'

"The actual conference was called to order in Buea on Monday, July 6, by elected chairman Basel Missionary Lutz. Using 2 Timothy 1:7 he reminded delegates of the indwelling Spirit who sustains amid all difficulties. He is also the instigator and implementor of Christ's love that indwells us for people whatever their condition may be, and however despised by others.

"Among goals and tasks to be considered were 1) cooperation and agreement concerning common activities and difficulties, 2) unfailing prayer and intercession for personal integrity toward one another and in the challenging sometimes problem-ridden Kamerun work, and 3) despite overwhelming schedules of work, keeping uppermost the care of souls. Schools, medical work, vocational efforts, etc., must subserve this primary task.

"Various representatives of the missions then presented the current status of their work which indicated progress despite many difficulties and hindrances. It was important that mission work be coordinated and goal-oriented. Fleeting ideas, personal preferences, and obsessions of home mission personnel should be discounted. Every missionary must keep in mind and be subservient to the comprehensive nature and program of the work. This is specially important in occupying new fields or founding new stations. To do so apart from cooperative decision-making is hazardous.

"On Tuesday, July 7, Presbyterian missionary Dr. Johnson referred to Acts 26:12 to remind us of personally experiencing Christ's presence. Paul had experienced Christ. Christ for him was no shadowy, mystical something but a living reality. Christ for Paul was the crucified, risen, ascended Lord for whom he joyfully and in faith applied himself and was therefore assured of victory.

"Practical matters this day included emphasizing the vernacular language. Exclusive stress on German on the mission schools could be perturbing. Even outside the missions more and more people felt that in the interests of both the colony and its natives the exclusive use of German was not desirable. Vernacular languages should be encouraged; doing so makes it easier to reach the hearts of people and to win them for Christ. The conference also felt more should be done in the way of practical helps to encourage people's becoming more useful and industrious. Industrial and agricultural ventures were seen as a means of nurturing personal development.

"Church discipline should be stressed. Church members should also learn to increase their financial support and to become personally more involved in church work.

"On July 8 Baptist Missionary Genz noted the practical significance of 2 Corinthians 4, namely, that God's messengers are commanded to share what they have seen and heard of the glory of Christ. This testimony is often given especially at times of physical and other problems. For all that, God wants us to so share in his Good News that his strength operates ever more increasingly in and through us to his glory.

"On the conference's final day attendees discussed several serious questions. For example, what makes reception of the Gospel difficult? For one thing, fear of evil spirits and of magic is a serious deterrent. The general fatalism of blacks is also a problem. Related to this fatalism is a lack of will for what is good that makes acceptance of salvation difficult. Often one hears: 'This is how God created me!' There is little perception of being a sinner who needs redemption. For effective preaching one must know and use the vernacular language and know peoples' manner of speaking and lifestyle. One should also know their sayings, fables, and fairy tales.

"The danger that natives regard baptism as something mystical, as some kind of wonder-working experience (this is influenced by

Catholic practice) must be prevented or corrected by basic teaching about the purpose of baptism.

"Spiritual nurturing must be increased. Missionaries unfortunately are so overburdened with other tasks that too little time remains for person to person ministry. Sinning against the seventh commandment is a kind of "heritage" which causes marriage problems. Christians need help in such situations.

"In strengthening the 'saints', simple preaching is important and should include many illustrations that 'click.' Prayer meetings should be enlivened by a variety of short, direct messages; prayer and music should be uplifting and meaningful.

"Infidelity is the only proper reason for divorce. Reconciliation should be pursued. Dismissal from church membership should be decided case by case. Polygamists cannot join the church unless they dismiss all but their first wife. If Christian women marry polygamists their church status must be decided case by case—is this a matter of free will or was it 'ancestor-arranged', etc. Sons may not marry their father's widow.

"The liquor problem must be vigorously met.

"In regard to enforced labor the missions agree that a certain amount of proper pressure is needed to develop a personal and national sense of work. If, however, workers are abused, missions and missionaries must protest. If the government does not respond, abuses should be made public.

"Before close of the Buea Conference the decision was made to prepare for the next such conference, possibly in two years. The happy and worthwhile days had passed only too quickly. While doctrinal differences and denominational affiliations had no place in the conference it greatly championed unity of purpose regarding evangelism. There was One in our midst, Bender's report observed, whose love united us, One for whom all our hearts beat in tune, and to whose service each of us rededicated ourselves."

(Signed)

C. J. Bender, Secy.

(According to a group picture nineteen Protestant missionaries—Basel, Presbyterian, Gozner, and Baptist—attended this initial conference.)

Permeating this initial all-evangelical Kamerun conference were significantly cooperative Christian assumptions and principles. Despite denominational differences, what prevailed were shared concerns of a theological and anthropological nature, as well as social, ethical, and evangelistic emphases. Its participants unitedly spoke of exclusive salvation in Christ. Witness to the risen Lord's self-disclosure, and to his promised presence, protection, and victory were unmistakable. However much a missionary's work might involve peril, trial, and affliction, he would nonetheless anticipate the final triumph of and exalt the Kingdom of God. Personal individual calling to serve Christ encompasses as well an awareness of shared comprehensive goals. Yet the missionary must not allow routine duties to erode time for one-on-one evangelistic and discipling ministry. The authority of Scripture and church discipline are not to be minimized. Clear biblical instruction reinforces monogamous marriage, a work ethic, and a distinctive Christian ethic including sobriety. Essential for confronting evil spirits, witchcraft, magic, and fatalism is dependence on the ascended and indwelling Christ.

Participants agreed that the prospect of another Kamerun all-evangelical conference in two years (1916) would reinforce the already present joyful sense of mutual engagement in divinely ordained work. Conviction was strong that God had launched a remarkable work in Kamerun; unprecedented channels of spiritual opportunity were already in place, moreover, that in the near future might eventuate and actually become a missions marvel in West Africa.

Missionaries attending 1914 Conference

10

DECLARATION OF WAR

The joys and anticipations of the 1914 Interdenominational Conference were short-lived, however. Troublesome situations in Duala had worsened since early rumbles of local tribal, commercial, political tensions and European power plays. During the closing years of Seitz's governorship and then those of Ebermeier and Gleim the resistance of Duala to colonial subservience had intensified to high-strung rebellion.

Berlin's encouragement of international business and influence at the expense of Kamerunians' local power and well-being needed to be faced. Chief Manga Bell had died in quiet trust of both Christian teaching and proper medical attention. To the amazement even consternation of pagan relatives no medicine man's potions had touched his lips. Son and heir Rudolf Manga Bell now became official Duala chief, spokesman and activist leader.

Plans for long-needed dredging and modernizing Duala harbor were well-received. Additional plans by Kamerun's Berlin-appointed governors and consuls to move—by force if necessary—natives and their homes from long-held central locations for distant resettlement was another matter. Officials' intentions to pay for land thus released riled natives on at least two counts; the price offered was too low; the land, in fact, by native tradition was theirs and thus not negotiable at any price. The 1884 contract of German-colonization had required inviolable perception of land use and ownership.

Response to the government's installing proper sanitation systems for the city's growing and specially European citizenry that would lessen malaria and other disease-abetting environments were generally accepted. Some Dualas allowed themselves to be relocated in keeping with such plans. Others who resisted saw their huts being deliberately destroyed and in protest fled for safety to the forests, there to harbor and deliberate on their grievances. The government used prisoners as well as forced laborers to tear down their fellow-natives' old dwellings and to build temporary huts in outlying areas. Military force was used as needed. Manga Rudolf Bell's protests characterized him increasingly as a radical, especially when he threatened to seek support for his people from known sympathizers overseas, including members of the press.

Secretly sending his secretary to activate public sentiment against Berlin's and Kamerun's officials' destabilizing practises in Africa succeeded in stopping anti-Duala operations, but only temporarily. On return home Manga Bell's secretary was imprisoned at once. Meanwhile Basel, Baptist and Catholic missionaries' efforts to at least limit the extent of divestiture of the Dualas' property, and despite their protesting charges of treason against Manga Bell and his secretary, the die seemed cast for worsening conditions. Bell was apprehended for possibly wanting to return Kamerun to England. Despite four years of efforts by Manga Bell to preserve his peoples' rights and dignity, he and his secretary were condemned to death for treason.

Collaborative sell-out, as it were, by Berlin and her colonial appointees to commercial and secular endeavors initiated a perhaps irreversible course of history for Kamerun. On August 9, 1914, Rudolf Manga Bell and secretary Ngoso Din were hanged.

Bitterness toward the Germans by Dualas was enormous. Bell's last words were: "I now part from my people, 'but damned be the Germans.' God, I beg you, hear my final request that this soil nevermore be trodden by Germans."

Basel missionary Vöhringer who accompanied Manga Bell on his final walk had no reply for this vindictive outburst. More tempered were the Chief's additional comments. Member of a Basel church—his wife was Baptist—Bell said: "I am sure that God will receive me in grace. I am dying for my fatherland (Kamerun)."

Said Vöhringer: "Manga Bell went to death as a Christian. As a last request he asked all those standing around to audibly join him in praying the Lord's prayer."

The wailing natives considered Manga Bell's death as murder by colonial powers that would be bitterly avenged in days to come.

Within days, on August 14, 1914, War was declared in Europe. By a month later on September 9, British warships entered Kamerun.

Not only Rudolf Manga Bell but also neighboring Kings Akwa and Deido had been offered the choice between supporting the colonial divestiture plans and what they involved, or totally losing their generations-old royal status and privileges as tribal rulers. Although not always on friendly terms, the three nonetheless joined forces in behalf of their beleaguered subjects. The either/or proposition given them required little deliberation.

The intensifying powder keg atmosphere already

mentioned in 1907 by then retiring Governor von Puttkamer would soon be verified by World War I. Both the French and British cited reasons, however, for ignoring the 1885 Treaty of Berlin that among other things stipulated that war in Europe was not to spill over to overseas colonies. Signed by delegates including the Queen of England and even then President Grover Cleveland of the United States, it was prefaced by a reference to Almighty God.

When war was declared in Europe, Kamerun missionaries and workers elsewhere in Africa and Asia therefore disbelieved that the conflict in Europe could affect their ministries. Britain's apparently accepted explanation for ignoring the Treaty's assurance of non-belligerence in colonies rested on the principle of so-called imperial defense. In a war with either Germany or France, she said, the neutrality clauses would favor either Germany or France but not her. Her usual practice in warring against a colonial power, therefore, would be simply to occupy overseas territory as quickly as possible and to use it as a kind of bargaining chip in peace negotiations. In any case the present European conflict was expected to be very short-lived.

The war's first shot was fired in German Togo at a German black by a British Gold Coast (Ghana) black. This pattern of white officers ordering blacks to fight other blacks became a frequent tactic in the Kamerun war arena. The number of black corpses and prisoners therefore obviously exceeded that of whites. At first natives were shocked to see whites, including benevolent missionaries, being dispossessed, imprisoned and interned by command of white military personnel. War being war, however, and for blacks not an infrequent experience, together with riling memories for them of land and property divestiture, added easily to racial and interracial disharmony. Especially appalling and aggrieving was the assignment of blacks by British and French whites to implement desired plundering and destruction of mission and other properties, not to mention physical violence and abuse of whites, including hundreds of missionaries.

> "...the campaign in the Cameroons was a toilsome business of nineteen months' duration....Few people unconnected with the West Coast of Africa had ever heard of the Cameroons before the year 1914....One lady who when told that a certain officer was in the Cameroons expressed a pious hope that he liked the regiment and would not catch a cold from wearing a kilt!" (Gorges, E. Howard, *The Great War in West Africa*, p.19).

11
MISSIONARY INTERNMENT

Only a few years earlier, even weeks, before the War, not only schools but also other aspects of mission work were in prime condition. Missions and their personnel anticipated a dramatically positive forward surge after difficult problem-ridden years of initial colonization.

The unprecedented Buea interdenominational conference of early July, 1914, had helped mitigate interpersonal and inter-group misunderstandings and power struggles. Four missions had attended: the Basel, American Presbyterian, German Baptist ,and Goszner, the last-named having just arrived in Kamerun. Overall reports and prospects were more than encouraging. Basel Mission, the largest and oldest of the four groups, showed growth on all fronts and would soon be penetrating inland areas. Part of its southern Kamerun territory it would probably transfer to the American Presbyterians who by comity arrangements concentrated their efforts in the south. Attendees at main Presbyterian stations often numbered 5,000 plus hundreds of baptismal candidates. Advances by them were under way as well as in adjunct New Kamerun. Their medical ministry served both blacks and Europeans, and an industrial program (shoemaking, carpentry, and basketry) had become self-supporting.

Like the Basel and Presbyterian work, that of the German Baptists also looked promising; churches, schools, and other efforts in the Duala district showed marked development. After ten years of hard endeavor, efforts among the Bassa and Banen tribes were finally taking hold as well. Christian impact was growing also around Fumban and near Jaunde where Islam was on the march.

As for Goszner Mission its four newly arrived workers had barely unpacked.

Beside Protestant development, that of Pallotine Mission Catholics was also evident.

All in all, more than 45,000 committed Christians and 20,000 catechumens were in the care and nurture of these Protestant and Catholic organizations. More than 250 missionaries (men and women) plus over 700 trained natives worked in over forty in stations and 800 subsidiary locations. The most productive work was through schools; at the beginning of 1914 over 50,000 students and trainees (mostly men but also women) were enrolled. A new era was dawning in Kamerun to win young people for Christ and imbue the colony with their influence. Government officials respected the work of mission schools and for several years contributed some financial support. They perceived the schools as not only a major means for spiritual and personal enlightenment of the people, but also for implementing the best of colonial intentions. In earlier years missionaries, unfortunately, often had to "win their way" for proper recognition of their role and positive influence. But now—by 1914—such problems were largely a thing of the past (except for War-related outbursts and situations). Participants in this July, 1914 Protestant Conference were therefore united in praise for progress already made and in hope and courage for what lay ahead.

In just a few short weeks, however, came the War. On

August 3 Kamerun Governor Karl Ebermeier issued regulations concerning the colony's minimal military forces. He announced, moreover, that German colonies and therefore Kamerun's missions were in no danger since Germany's confrontation involved only France and Russia. Nevertheless, when Britain still in August entered the War the balance of power changed for colonial and commercial clout in Africa. In doing so Britain had preemptorially negated its signing of the 1907 Hague Agreement that in case of war signatory colonial powers would not make pawns of their colonies.

With the prompt arrival of British and French warships and ongoing deployment of troops the War soon criss-crossed Kamerun and other German colonies as well. The rapidity with which the missions' glowing prospect of continuing wholesome development changed under the War's destructive sweep is almost beyond belief. In less than a year after September 14, 1914's surrender of Duala and that of capitol city Buea in November, almost all missionaries were gone. Replacing them were black and white British and French military, political, government, and business personnel of diverse motivations. Fortunately, four appointees of the Paris Evangelical Mission Society, namely, Pastor Allégret of the Paris Evangelical Church and Chaplain of the French Army now assigned to Kamerun; Missionary Bergeret, former missionary in New Hebrides and New Caledonia; Missionary Ochsner de Coninck, retired from Basuto Mission; and Missionary Christol of Zambesi arrived to help and to reorganize Kamerun's confused War-orphaned people and enterprises.

Only the American Benders of Berlin's German Baptist Society, and for three years the Australian Rohdes of Basel Mission, were allowed to remain in Kamerun, but only under imposed restrictions and often subject to unseemly treatment. Ongoing problems of lack of food, clothing, medical supplies, salary, communication with native workers, and uncertainties about far away children shadowed the days, months, and years. But always *over*shadowing such human concerns was the omnipotent, omniscient, and omnipresent God, Ruler of men and nations and coming King of kings and Lord of lords.

Faith in that same God sustained also absent fellow-workers who were thrust from long standing, hard won mission stations into deceptive internment and imprisonment. The Allies' promise to release missionaries after they simply signed their names at a Duala hospital was surely among the greatest lies of so-called civilized officials. Ready and waiting for takeoff after registration were quay-side warships that scooped up the workers for imprisonment in England, France, and Spain via stops at notorious labor camps.

Although the Allies did not so identify them, missionaries considered their stations and homes as neutral places of peace and ministry. It was not uncommon for enemy personnel to curse Christian enterprises and their workers. The loudest and vilest were not necessarily the most dangerous, however. One day Bender called on a newly appointed Buea official and invited him to tea in Soppo. "I don't care a hoot about missions," he answered. "You don't need to," replied Bender. "I didn't come to see you because you're British or not British, but as a friend and neighbor. You don't need to visit the mission as such but simply me as a fellow human being." "If," Bender continued, "you had bad experiences with missionaries in India, why not try one in Africa?" "McD.," as it developed, was actually the son of a Scottish minister and brother of a respected Anglican priest. Although he called himself the black sheep of the family, McD. was, in fact, a good fellow at heart and in time did the Benders and the Baptist mission many a good turn and in good spirit, too.

The few Germans allowed to remain at their posts for a short time nevertheless lost all their possessions and their freedom as well. Even people from neutral countries were treated like enemies and led away as prisoners. One would have thought that at least the Swiss (Basel) missionaries' rights would have been respected, but they, in fact, suffered the worst treatment of all and the greatest losses.

Allied abuses such as dragging native women into churches to rape them, or riding horses into chapels to befoul the altars, seem pale by today's technologically implemented atrocities. Be that as it may, the motivation and power source for both the earlier crude practices and today's sophisticated horrors are probably the same. Rowdiness and lawlessness prevailed. Both whites and blacks plundered, looted, and destroyed mission properties, burned valuable records and books, manhandled and robbed missionaries, and captured and delivered them to authorities for posted booty.

On November 15, 1914, Sunday morning church services at Soppo had just finished when young people came shouting, "The English are coming! The English are coming!" The Benders and house guest Missionary Genz on sick leave from Duala had been apprised of this possibility for several weeks. They had, in fact, recently mounted several flags at the Baptist Mission gate, one white Cross-emblazened Christian flag to symbolize peace and noncombatance and one faded red, white, and blue Old Glory to announce American citizenship and protection.

This Lord's day morning about one hundred black soldiers with bayonets found grassy lounging spots near the mission to await straggler forces. Several men began sketching maps of the compound to use in a possible search for hidden ammunition or even native spies. With special glasses another soldier climbed and sat in one of Bender's roadside trees to survey and report on overall compound activities. Perhaps most foreboding, however, was the guard posted at the mission gate to check Bender's comings and goings.

Major Rose and his remaining contingent finally arrived from their march on Tiko. Having assured himself of his waiting men's fulfillment of various responsibilities, he approached Bender and Genz standing nearby, and with hardly another word requested lunch for himself and his officers.

Mrs. Bender's ever-ready kitchen and graciousness filled the bill. At table Rose and Bender soon found themselves discussing current Kamerun affairs and doing so, moreover, in a manner that intimated further associations sometime, somewhere. That same day, November 15, after militarily negligible inroads on Soppo, Rose and his men moved toward Buea. The capital city had actually already surrendered after a series of incursions on surrounding Mt. Kamerun villages. Over 170 Germans, including sixty-eight women and children, had been taken prisoner at Buea and removed to Duala. Thus far the total number of captured Germans was 1200, many of them noncombatant missionaries who in time were deported to British or other prisons.

Europeans in the Buea-Soppo area were taken away in two lots. So far the Benders seemed safe enough. But when a friend told them they were on a list for deportation in two days, Bender jumped into action. Inquiry at Buea verified his friend's warning. He therefore had authorities check his officially filed papers who found them in good order. Bender reminded them that as an American, a citizen of a neutral country, he therefore could not be treated like a prisoner without grave abuse of international law. The upshot of this dialogue was that while Bender was not a prisoner, he could not remain unguarded in Soppo.

Shocking reports of seizure in the Duala area of missionaries for internment and imprisonment had been troubling Bender. Perhaps, he thought, he ought to return to Duala, his former work domain from 1899 to 1909 to be of help and perhaps even superintend the entire Kamerun Baptist work the best he could. At least he could try. From British officials now replacing former familiar German staff he therefore requested permission to travel. Years of overseas experience reminded him to secure as well, assorted signed and stamped permits and passes for negotiating unforeseen emergencies or now, if necessary, War-related dilemmas. He also exchanged German for British money. While waiting for government response to these requests the Benders could now mothball, as it were, their Soppo quarters and entrust to trained Kamerunians the spiritual care of their people and the safe-keeping of their beloved Soppo.

Forwarded to Duala, Bender's Buea requests were granted by the Political Officer who also gave permission to stay at the Duala Baptist Mission. Bender had to first get a travel pass to Victoria, however, to catch the last November 26th Duala-bound prisoner transport. The word "prisoner" set off a veritable alarm in Bender's mind. He at once challenged the Buea officer. "You're an Englishman, I'm an American," said Bender. "Both of us are equally proud of our status. If you were in my place," Bender continued, "would you allow yourself to be transported with prisoners and under military control?" "Under no circumstances," came the reply. "Neither do I," said Bender.

Granting him now a special pass to travel to Victoria whenever he wished and with whatever luggage, the Buea official, with a "Well, have I done enough for you?" still reminded Bender about prompt boarding of the Victoria vessel to Duala.

After giving away his poultry and cows (he had taught the cowherd how to milk) Bender made a list of all his household and other items to file at Buea offices. If plundering occurred during their absence the Benders could then appeal, if need be, for proper reimbursement.

The night before departure Bender put books and records in order and locked them away. At daybreak he went once more to visit faithful helper Mwafise who lay dying in his hut, and with a prayer closed his co-worker's eyes. Having seen Mrs. Bender off by train (she was several months pregnant with daughter Helga), Bender accompanied by porters carrying items that could not go by train, then walked the twenty-two kilometers to Victoria.

From Victoria, Hedwig and he travelled on freighter "Haussa," one of many vessels seized from the Hamburg Woermann merchants at the beginning of the War. Men were put on open deck above the hatch, wives and children under the sundeck on the starboard deck and in cabins where there was room. Since the Benders were not prisoners and had so indicated to the transport officer, they were taken to the Captain's cabin where the ship's machinist who had been to America regaled them with his experiences there.

Having arrived at Duala, only the Benders who

thought that all passengers were being brought to Duala, were put ashore. Not so. With the Benders dropped off, the "Haussa" continued at once into Kamerun's main harbor to anchor near prisoner transport "Appen." Meanwhile, porters at Duala were taking the Benders into the city and, presumably, directly to the Baptist Mission. Instead they found themselves in short order in the city prison. Apparently they were prisoners, or at least being treated as such. Strange to say, Bender had completely forgotten he had in his pocket a letter of recommendation to the Political Officer. This helped not a whit, however, since the PO had been informed about the Benders' coming and had himself made all arrangements regarding their stay.

Shocked by this turn of events, Bender could hardly control himself. Confrontation would hardly have helped, however. Bender decided to wait, to see what would develop. There was no reason to challenge the prison sergeant for he was simply following orders. On leaving Soppo, Exodus 33:14 had reminded Bender, "My presence shall go with thee."

The following day when Bender looked up the PO, he discovered there had been a change of officers. Told to return in a few days to see about living at the Mission, Bender did so but was met by yet another officer. From him he learned that he could not go to the German Baptist Mission because the French objected. That was as good as being told, "Leave Kamerun and go home." For Bender such a notion of forced return to America was impossible. He felt he must do whatever he could to preserve and reinforce the Mission and its work. He therefore requested return to Soppo! What was more, if this request were denied, he would demand first class passage for his wife and himself to New York via Liverpool on one of the regular passenger ships. The prison ship "Appam" still lay ominously at anchor. Bender's newest and unexpected request was therefore sent at once to the Political Officer who checked Bender's papers yet another time.

The following day when the "Appam" with its prisoners lifted anchor, Bender knew his request had been accepted in one way or another. Word came, in fact, that he could return to Soppo. The Benders could truly say, "Hitherto the Lord has helped." They were not concerned about remaining in Kamerun under War conditions and were willing and ready to work however necessary to provide essential food supplies. In his pocket, moreover, Bender still had the receipt for items surrendered at Soppo and now prepared a statement of estimated value for the Political Officer. He had misgivings about getting the requested funds because the Soppo receipt had been made out to the German Baptist Mission and not to him personally. But God knew the Benders needed this money, especially since they were totally cut off from all former connections and sources of help and support and would continue to be so.

Various officers checked out Bender's request for about 2600 German marks and found it reasonable. There would still be the treasurer to contend with for several days for he would issue the actual money. Once again God intervened. Instead of receiving the money in several allotments as had been indicated, Bender was paid in one lump sum and that, moreover, in British money.

Bender therefore quickly inquired about transport back to Victoria. Before steamer departure, however, he would need to purchase supplies and even before that, would need to secure approval by the military of his shopping list. Although the Buea Political Officer had reassured him about getting whatever he needed in Duala, especially food, Bender was disappointed; the military disallowed his shopping requests. Having learned that the Victoria steamer was departing an hour late, Bender told himself that if he were indeed a free man he should therefore be able to function as one. He therefore boldly proceeded to the commissary and soon gathered whatever he needed. As far as the merchants were concerned, anyone with the right kind and amount of money was welcome.

While the Benders' prison stay proved shorter than it might have been, it still was an invaluable test of faith and patience. Prison rations had been a small loaf of bread per day (sometimes a moldy grey-green), a tin of sardines or herring, some rancid margarine, and if the kitchen staff didn't drink it themselves, some tea or coffee.

Occasionally they had some Australian corned beef. For all that, the Benders knew that they fared far better than those starving in Europe because of food blockades. Their friendly black prison attendant, moreover, not only supplemented the Benders' meager fare with some of his own food—and he didn't have much—but on their departure even gave them some helpful household items.

The most difficult aspect of Benders' imprisonment was being unable to worship and fellowship with black fellow believers. They could see the tips of church steeples, could hear the call of bells, and the singing of hymns borne on the wind, but they were prisoners and guarded like criminals. Permission to see or speak with American missionary colleagues interned nearby was also denied. "Not now," was the answer. Before Benders knew it, their co-workers were on the high seas toward further imprisonment elsewhere: they had refused to lie about incriminating evidence against their captors.

The Benders' return trip to Victoria co-mingled joys, sorrows, and apprehensions. The ship's captain was cordial enough, but somewhere and somehow during the trip valuable possessions of the missionaries were stolen, including Bender's one and only suitcoat. Journey's end, moreover, found the returnees engulfed in tropical darkness with no place to spend the night except an abandoned empty shack. However emotionally drained by their experiences in Duala and weary of body, they nonetheless were buoyed by the prospect of their Soppo home and resuming life and work among their people.

Arriving the next day at the train station, the Benders encountered a newly arrived troop of soldiers. Everything was confusion. Weary of waiting for the transport officer to end his noon siesta, Bender proceeded to the official's lodgings to speed up clearance of his baggage. On a small table in the foyer Bender saw, of all things, his own bunch of assorted keys that on leaving Soppo he had turned over to the government! He could hardly believe his eyes! God had cared for his workers even in this last detail.

The first night back in their home was hardly uneventful. Around midnight, noise on the front veranda wakened Bender. On checking he found two black soldiers breaking the windows. The previous night, as later reported by neighbors, the same men had stolen costly blankets and linens; now they had returned to continue their looting. Had the Benders not returned to Soppo at just this time, everything in their home would very likely have been plundered as had been the case at Basel and other mission stations. Bender warded off the thieves just before they entered Mrs. Bender's bedroom. Such intrusion would have been shocking indeed. Bender filed charges against the known culprits but officials did nothing to return the stolen goods or even to discipline the thieves.

Word of the Benders' return spread like wildfire. People kept coming all the next day to greet them. Some who had bought small items from the missionaries when they left now returned them. Others brought food from their own meager supplies. Even some friendly and sympathetic British helped in various ways. As the months moved toward Christmas, ten kilos of flour came from Major Rose, and an assortment of meats from the feisty Mr. McD. From now on the struggle for survival would intensify. Since Duala was off limits for the Benders and Victoria shops were closed, the Benders would often have been in dire straits without the help of African Christians who were free to secure supplies themselves or through friends and relatives.

Food prices especially at the beginning of the War were unbelievable, sometimes triple or quadruple the usual rate. Clothing was equally expensive and of poor quality. Occasionally black mission helpers secured things for Benders at good prices through the Officers' PX. At times they bought things from homeward-bound English and French. For a short while supplies were available from the Basel Mission at the Gold Coast (Ghana). When freight service resumed between New York and West Africa, the Benders sometimes got supplies through this avenue. In July, 1918, foodstuffs were once again everywhere in very short supply; all Europeans in the British sector were, in fact, put on rations (the French rationed throughout the entire war). During this time Bender received help from the American Presbyterian missionaries who lovingly shared some of their food.

In early 1919 there was once again great scarcity of flour; it was unavailable anywhere for any amount of money. Out of this dilemma the Benders were helped by their French and British sailor friends who periodically docked in Duala or Victoria and enjoyed coming to Soppo for relaxing visits or stays with the Benders.

Despite the war, mission work among the Mt. Kamerun Bakwiri people experienced little interruption. Early on there had been problems about visiting mission outstations since soldiers for some reason identified anyone not wearing khaki kneepants as being German. Once on a trip to Victoria, Bender passed the Soppo railroad station where a guard was posted. Paying no attention to him Bender passed the building when he heard a shrill "Stop!" behind him. Turning, he saw several captains talking to an excited soldier who had breathlessly run up to them and announced, "Massa, a German done pass for road!" The "German" was wearing long trousers. In time soldiers came to recognize Bender, however, and allowed him freedom of movement.

Fortunately Bender had a special travel pass. About a year after he had received it, he got the following query from a Buea Political Officer:

> Mr. Bender, Soppo
> Sir:
> Will you please inform me by whose authority you are traveling about this district and the extent of your peregrinations?
> I have the honor to be, Sir,
>
> > Your obedient servant
> > A.H.D.P.

When Bender thereupon showed the said A.H.D.P. his pass and a map of his mission territory, he was allowed to travel in his extended Soppo district whenever and wherever he pleased. Actually this "obedient servant" who was now in Soppo had himself given Bender this right to travel in Duala shortly before Bender's return to Soppo! Bender had asked him there: "Will I be permitted to carry out my mission work unhindered, including traveling?" To this the officer had answered, "I wouldn't know what should hinder you to do your work in the usual way. But let me advise you to take care in your dealings with the natives." He should rather have added, "Beware of the deliberate change, interchange, and exchange of Political Officers."

Among those who had been similarly maligned because of missionary engagement was Reinhold Rohde. It was interesting, in fact, that both he and Bender would be ordained, as it were, to encourage and help each other in Soppo.

From January to October, 1914, Rohde, born in Australia and a citizen of that country, had managed to maintain his inland Basel Mission station. His British connection was of little consequence to authorities, however. When his station was attacked and his personal effects examined the military inspector simply asked: "What shall I do with this bloke? Shall we take his money, too?" This situation was yet another sample of many Allies' enmity against Christianity and missions.

When led away from his station Rohde had had to surrender most of his possessions but received no receipt. Perhaps as a British subject Rohde should have insisted from the beginning on keeping his goods or at least on receiving a receipt for them. In any case, having arrived in Duala with almost nothing to his name, he heard General Dobell say: "We can have no useless mouths to feed. If he cannot support himself, let him go home." Oddly enough, the Buea Political Officer just then in Duala had heard the General's comment and suggested in his brusque way, "Why don't you go to Bender in Soppo?"

In the meantime, Bender had received a message from the helpful Political Officer now returned to Buea:

Honorable Mr. Bender:

Today I received a telegram from Duala with a request to ask if you would be willing to receive an English missionary by the name of Rohde, and his wife and child. I am requested to reply by telegraph. Would you be so kind as to let me know if you are favorably disposed?

Yours truly,

B.W.S., PO

In view of Bender's positive reply Missionary Rohde and his family arrived in Soppo on January 4, 1915, and lived with the Benders until October 9, 1917, when Rohde was arrested, brought to Victoria, and five days later brought to England as a prisoner. The reason for such treatment can only be conjectured. On December 7, 1916, Rohde and Bender were ordered to appear before a yet another of frequently changing Resident Ministers at Buea. Passports were checked, and oral statements were requested of the missionaries' personal losses because of the War.

Weeks later written confirmation of previously oral statements was requested. Bender suspected that something was being instigated against Rohde and himself and so was careful in stating his claims. The December 29 notice to Bender read as follows:

Sir: From our record of December 7 concerning conversations in my office I take it that you have no complaints to file against the local authorities, and that the only unfortunate incident was damage to your potato patch by troops on December 14. Would you please indicate whether this statement is correct?

Yours—

E.C.D., Resident of Cameroons Province

Bender had really wanted to again mention also the break-in of soldiers into his residence and the stealing of blankets, linens, etc., but thought it wiser not to do so. He therefore confirmed the Resident's current statement but only on the basis of an express government request and not as some kind of a "claim" for payment of damages. His passport being criticized because of its 1904 date, Bender indicated the exception made for American missionaries by a 1911 law that validated his passport despite its age. When Bender inquired about the location of the nearest American consul in West Africa the passport problem was quickly dropped. Thereafter Bender was troubled only once more in this way.

He was summoned to Buea to appear before the police commissioner and to bring his papers. Copies made of these were then sent to Lagos. Bender's suspicion that secret agencies were once again at work was confirmed several days later through a strange dream.

In this dream Bender was followed by a lion just as he emerged from the Soppo church. When just ready to pounce on him the lion disappeared into thin air. In the lion's place a wild boar suddenly appeared. Bender tried to hide from it behind a rock. Coming close to the rock the boar then just stood there as if transfixed. To Bender's surprise, its features changed into those of the Buea Resident, but then vanished, as had the lion, into thin air. To Bender this was more than just a dream—it was a real incident, one that in fact strengthened his faith. Bender now knew that the conspiracy against him would be frustrated. At the same time he also knew he must be careful.

A week later Bender received the following communication from Buea, written in German:

To Missionary Bender
Your Reverence:
I should like to speak regarding a very urgent situation under four eyes only and to ask a convenient time for this. I am a clerk in the present Resident's office. Here at this time the matter of your remaining in Kamerun during the War time is being discussed. To insure my safety I would like to ask you to promise not to betray me. Because of the urgency of the matter and because of the absence of other preoccupations just now it seems well-timed to suggest such a meeting. May I further request an eventual compensation? Do not worry. Receive my respectful regards—
N. N.
I am prepared to appear there at any time.
Reply through messenger.

Bender was more than puzzled. What should he do? Was this a trap of some kind? Was the writer sincere? What bothered Bender most of all was the secrecy of all this and the messenger's abuse of his trust as an employee. He was put off as well by the suggested remuneration for proffered services. Bender therefore replied—in English—that he appreciated the gentleman's concern for him. He was not troubled, however, since he was in the service of a Lord without whose permission not a hair of his head could fall. As far as Bender was concerned, that was the end of the matter, and so it was apparently, for Bender neither saw nor heard anything more about the situation.

Missionary Rohde had trouble, too, because of his old passport. His British citizenship, moreover, was disputed. He had to appear in Buea before a commission chaired, in fact, by the High Commissioner of Nigeria about his statements concerning personal losses. These statements, it seems, were interpreted as complaints against government authorities. Both British and French military officers had brought charges against him. Rumors, in fact, were circulating that Rohde must soon leave the colony. A newly arrived Buea Resident informed Rohde that the Governor General of Nigeria, Sir Frederic Lugard, was demanding Rohde's immediate departure; he was no longer welcome.

In August, 1917, Rohde therefore petitioned the Governor General in Lagos in defense of his rights as a British subject, and insisted on the right to be told the specific reason of charges against him; he also requested the right to defend himself. At the same time because of the climatic hazards of an ocean voyage at that season, especially with three small children, Rohde asked permission to remain in Kamerun. He waited in vain for an answer. Meanwhile, rumors spread that the Rohdes were being forced to leave with the next ship.

The evening of October 8, 1917, as darkness fell, the unheard-of happened: the police commissioner appeared with four soldiers to arrest Mr. Rohde. The black soldiers who stayed the night as security were arrogant and bold. Forcing themselves into the bedroom where Mrs. Rohde was with the three children, they even poked around in boxes and trunks. Missionary Rohde finally threw them out.

It was a sad night for everyone. The following day was even more so. At two in the afternoon Missionary Rohde and his family under military escort left Soppo Mission station where he had spent almost three happy and work-productive years, and where two of his children were born. Through Rohde's being led away the Basel

Mission was robbed of its last Kamerun worker and a thriving mission enterprise was totally cancelled.

The Benders' feelings were beyond belief. Parting from these colleagues with whom they had shared through thick and thin was difficult, to say the least. Especially appropriate for this sad day was Hebrews 11:16: "They look for a better country for God has prepared for them a city."

Despite their fortunate and happy Soppo accommodations and fellowship with the Benders, the Rohdes' survival experiences during that period were not easy. With the addition of two Soppo-born children, their family now numbered five persons of whom the three children needed milk every day. Surely the seventy-five cattle at nearby Buea dairy could meet that need. When Rohde asked permission of the Political Officer to buy milk, the answer was: "We have too many calves to feed; calves are better than babies. People have no business having babies out here." It was sad, certainly humiliating, for Rohde to be treated thus by a fellow Briton simply because he, Rohde, was a missionary. While he was grudgingly given a small amount of milk from time to time, one day Rohde was told he could have no more.

The black dairy supervisor was beside himself when forbidden to sell neither Rohde nor Bender any dairy products whatsoever. "That's terrible," said the black dairyman, "small children surely need milk!" In time a sympathetic black neighbor loaned Rohde two African cows that every day supplied several liters of milk. It should be noted that the successor to the mean-spirited Political Officer was as friendly as his predecessor had been vindictive. In other words, Rohde and Bender through the years were constantly at the mercy of vacillating situations that reflected the differing personalities, convictions and/or prejudices of British and French officialdom.

Ousted, homeless, and penniless in 1914 from his Kamerun mission station, Rohde had wondered, "What now? Where shall I stay?" God's answer had turned out to be an entrustment to Rohde of several years of Basel ministry in the Soppo extended area, and accommodations with the Baptist Benders. Now in 1917, uprooted again, this time from Soppo security and ministry, Rohde faced the same questions as before: "What now? Where shall I live?" Just as God's assigning him to Soppo had been by an alert, unknown Political Officer, so now another "surprise agent" would locate Rohde in London housing and ministry fellowship.

Because of the war, Rohde was disallowed to travel to Basel Mission Headquarters in Switzerland. He was similarly disallowed return to Australia, his birthplace and home. Was it mere happenstance now that he unexpectedly met Missionary Cooper on a busy London street? Another yet earlier link in God's chain of loving care was Rohde's having already met Cooper, and in Soppo of all places, when the Coopers were guests in the Benders' R&R program. Now in London the men were therefore meeting not as strangers but as friends.

Shortly before his forced removal from Kamerun to England, Rohde had officially ordained two native pastors to maintain and strengthen the Basel work he left behind. Some of Bender's trained and in time also ordained workers would be similarly involved in takeover of Baptist work. Such entrustment of native leadership was essential for preserving and enlarging the patient, hard-won "pioneer" ministries of white "career" missionaries. Sown at the Edinburgh Mission Conference of 1910, small seeds of coming national, political, and religious independence, not to mention changes in mission philosophy and practice, took root during World War I and its subsequent years.

The unexpected arrest and deportation of Rohde and other Protestant missionaries was a hard blow for orphaned churches, especially when war conditions of economic, moral, and social laxity carried a resurgence of paganism and cultism. In the absence of white missionaries, growing confusion and insubordination among native Christians and workers soon threatened church stability and significance.

Aware of Rohde's and others' deportation, one of Bender's younger but promising Duala-assigned workers wrote him in Soppo:

> Dear Sir:
>
> You can't imagine how happy we are that you are here. We grieve deeply that the other missionaries have been taken away. We constantly pray that God will soon return them to us. We sense increasingly that without the missionaries' help we are not doing too well. You yourself know us Africans. For a little while everything is fine; then everyone wants to be number one and wants to be in charge. The missionaries always kept things in good order so that the work progressed.

It was the older and therefore respected and accepted elders of both Basel and Baptist churches who then stepped in to help restore church order and stability. As best he could, Bender similarly visited extended Soppo, Buea, and even Victoria-related villages and Christians, not all of them necessarily Baptist. At nearby Catholic centers, non-interned teachers and seminarians were always glad to see him. They bombarded him with questions about current affairs and jumped with joy to be handed a letter from their absent padres. At nearby plantations Bender also sought out Presbyterians working far from their homes and churches. Maintaining interdenominational fellowships and concerns initiated at the pre-War 1914   Buea Interdenominational Conference became increasingly meaningful and important for demonstrating the strength of Christian life and witness in a growingly turbulent society and world.

Imprisonment and deportation of the missionaries was a blow to many black Christians and engendered in them feelings of despair and uncertainty. Worsening stresses and strains and anxieties nonetheless brought about a searching after God, a desire for spiritual renewal and release from the fear of perdition. More than ever evangelistic outreach was needed and carried forward. A great spiritual harvest time ensued. Hundreds were added to churches in the first years of the war. Those Christians who had gone into hiding returned in time to their villages. Contrary to what had been noised abroad by officials, God's work was in no sense finished.

True, of the 150 European mission workers (mostly Basel, Baptist, Goszner, or Catholic), only Rohde and Bender remained. Protected by their American affiliation the American Presbyterians had been allowed to stay. The arrival of the Paris Protestant Missionary Society missionaries was timely and effective in lending leadership and giving counsel.

Carl and Hedwig Bender

12
LONDON AND BEYOND

The Quakers stressed variously accepted or rejected principles, namely: 1) Christian missions should be international, even supranational endeavors, *not* politically-oriented. 2) Because cutting off mission work for even a short time leads to diminution or loss of such ministry and is difficult to resume, consideration should be given to establishing a special kind of commission. Composed of government and mission representatives of various countries, such a group could establish and help implement ways of returning missionaries to their fields from a supernational and supranational perspective of work, and not one regulated, as currently, by governmental or private motivations.

This mindset daily propelled Quaker humanitarianism toward multiple thousands of war-victimized people, whatever their race, creed, citizenship, or country of origin. Such legendary loving provision in London and by extension elsewhere of food, shelter, clothing, travel, counsel, and spiritual concern rescued individuals and families from despair and even death. This Quaker spirit jumped manmade geographical hurdles to kindle cooperative programs in even enemy terrain. People from Africa, Asia, the Continent, the United

States, and elsewhere who experienced merciful assistance by the Quakers often, in turn, themselves became ambassadors of humanitarian thinking and activity.

Through Cooper's aforementioned Quaker-related help in London, Missionary Rohde and his family soon experienced and then themselves emulated the Friends' practical philosophy. Having completed six years of ministerial training at Basel on the basis of entrance requirements of a sound conversion experience and an authentic call to missions, Rohde in time would until 1917 become a revered worker in German Kamerun despite his Australian birth and British citizenship.

On October 8, 1917, the Rohdes, as part of a contingent of fourteen ships, undertook a seemingly mysterious voyage, destination unknown. On November 22, after avoidance of fearsome submarines, the family landed at Tilbury on the Thames River. The very next day they were searched by the military and checked out by Scotland Yard, who declared them free and at liberty. Facing the question, "Where will we live?" as he did on expulsion from his Kamerun mission station, he now found God's answer among the Quakers. Through them Rohde and his family house-sat a large building and its tenants until its owner returned from Switzerland in 1918 to reclaim her property. So again the search for lodgings began. This time the move was to a large hall in a Lutheran Church, a transition that shortly led to Rohde's pastoring two Lutheran churches on opposite sides of London whose German pastors had been expelled. The salary was a British pound per day.

Finally in December, 1920, the Rohde family, now enlarged by a London-born fourth daughter and a first son, sailed from Liverpool to Australia to a widowed mother and other patiently waiting family and friends.

After an extended period as a dearly beloved pastor, Rohde and his wife moved for retirement into a home specially bought for them by a now married daughter Tabitha—who had been born in Soppo and had resided there with her parents and the Benders, including playmate Helga—and Tabitha's husband, Dr. Edwin G. Tscharke AO MBE. (See End Note).

London and Britain in general faced the unforeseen problem of defining who of its citizens and population, including visitors and tourists, were subject to imprisonment, travel restrictions, food rationing, and other pronouncements. Being an island subject on all sides to attack made customary returns to the United States, for example, of students, tour groups, performing artists, visiting scientists, professors, etc. , difficult to say the least. Non-British spouses; longstanding foreign non-citizens; German chefs, tailors, and hotel staff, not to mention a vast number of German business and technical people; and even the King's baker—all were subject to checking and classifying. Even loyal British having German-sounding surnames were suspect. (At one point in the war British royalty assumed the House of Windsor identity and also changed their German von Battenberg connections to Mountbatten.)

People retained for English supervision were assigned to camps of varying suitability and for a time, even to ships. In these accommodations the mix of internees was not necessarily made according to similarity of age, social status, race, interest, and lifestyles. The terrible boredom of being incarcerated with nothing to do was finally remedied by providing musical instruments, craft materials, newspapers, books, and other diversionary items.

At Lancaster camp, an old wagon factory herded 700

men in one large room. On the race course at Newbury prisoners were housed in horse stalls, four to six men in each. In other camps men confined in barbed wire enclosures for as long as four years succumbed to mental breakdown called "barbed wire disease." On the Isle of Man, Knockaloe Camp, comprised of separate compounds wired off from each other, including one used for a cemetery, was probably the most horrendous and shocking confinement center of all. It housed 23,000 men. (People who could afford to pay the government a weekly sum, it should be noted, could be settled in special "camps" located in beautiful parks. (See End Note.)

How men in these many scattered camps were clothed and fed and how their wives and children were cared for is another story in itself. All in all, St. Stephen's workers registered at least 30,000 "case studies." Of these at least 1,000 pertained to missionaries from Africa, India, and elsewhere. Among them were the Kamerun missionaries whom Bender in 1914 had seen shipped from Duala, and of whom the Benders could easily have been a part. Seized and incarcerated without warning, they had only the clothes on their backs, tropical clothing at that, no money—it was forcibly taken from them—and in fact no possessions of any kind.

While the men were interned in London for questioning and were separated from their wives and children, families faced a double kind of prison experience. For wives and children, visits to clothes closets, securing housing, and providing food became immediate problems. Here again the Friends were prepared to help. Although, like their husbands, the wives were considered "prisoners of war," they were kept comfortably safe though isolated while the Friends' Emergency Committee helped arrange travel for them to Germany. Husbands meanwhile remained in camps. If they were ordained ministers they were repatriated after one to four months of imprisonment. If they were industrial missionaries they were detained throughout the war.

Just as Britain returned German prisoners to Germany in due course, so Germany returned its interned British to England. This constructive reciprocal arrangement was another phase of the Quakers' work. In a shared perception of international and supranational philosophy, similar aid committees functioned throughout the war in both Britain and Germany.

13

WAR'S END 1916

With a population of almost 3,000,000 natives and 2,000 Europeans, 1700 of them Germans, Kamerun at outbreak of World War I covered about 300,000 square miles. Start-up British and French fighting troops each numbered about 3,000 plus military officers. Consisting largely of Africans from their or other Europeans' colonies such as Nigeria, the Gold Coast, Congo, Gabon, Sierra Leone, Gambia, and even India, Allied reenforcements were available close at hand. As for Germany, its fighting forces in Kamerun included 200 officers, 2,000 native troops, and 60 German plus 1,500 native armed police.

Except by the educated elite, West Africans generally did not differentiate much between the British, French, and German colonial systems; practice and procedures in these systems seemed to them to be similar or dissimilar depending on variable factors. For many, if not most natives, the developing question had become not which colonial rule to prefer, but rather how to eliminate it.

At present, especially disaffected toward Germans because of their imposed divestiture of land and village resettlements, not to mention the hanging of their hero Manga Bell, the Dualas might be perceived by the English and French as rather easy game. That Manga's nephew

William Bell and his friends helped arriving enemies negotiate their ships to safe harbor-piers evidenced at least some measure of the Dualas' turncoating. In any case, the war could possibly be short, even if not necessarily sweet.

The "Cameroon Campaign" (to use the British appellation) began in late August, 1914, after a short takeover of neighboring Togo. Under the well-directed troops of Duala-stationed Brigadier General Charles Dobell, Inspector General of the *West African Frontier Force*, and those of General Aymerich headquartered in Brazzaville, Congo, and those of Brigadier General Cunliffe's famous *Nigeria Regiment*, devastating military strikes hammered Kamerun at seven different north, south, east, and west battle fronts.

Their plan to decimate the extended Duala, Victoria, and Buea areas, and in that order, was largely successful. Only one or two more military encounters were needed to confirm the Allies' prowess. One would be a disappointing surprise, the other a maze of martial endurance.

By February, 1915, German military resistance especially in south Kamerun had apparently given up. With their thorough-going extended Duala, Victoria, and Buea campaigns a decided success, the British and French forces now envisioned taking Jaunde as their plum. Developed by commercially and politically expansionist Governor Puttkamer, the city gained swift credence as an essential key to Kamerun's future (now the nation's capital). Successive explorers and missionaries as well, especially the Presbyterians, perceived the Jaunde area as significant for both its natural resources and no less its accessibility to yet unreached tribes.

Duala's cross-country trade network already in place together with Jaunde's nearby Congo markets boded well for both national and international commerce. Recognizing

Jaunde's importance, regiments of Generals Dobell, Aymerich, and Cunliffe therefore contemplated a cooperative take-over of the city and its people. To converge on this target from three different locations over diverse terrain at approximately the same time represented herculean skill, let alone hope.

As originally planned, Duala, Victoria, Buea, and their related or adjacent areas had been conquered. Now the generals, each one with his own and adjutant military forces, would trek varying distances to their already perceived new Kamerun headquarters. By January 1, 1916, Dobell had reached and overtaken Jaunde. On January 8 and 9 the others joined him—Cunliffe's troops had marched six hundred miles, Aymerich's people, one thousand. All they found in Jaunde were two or three people, and nothing by way of food or drink.

The Germans and natives had crossed the border to the safety of neutral Spanish Muni 130 miles away. Thousands of Kamerunians, 6,000 of them soldiers and many even sick and wounded, had eluded the Allies. Here, together with Kamerun Governor Ebermeier and his military commander Colonel Zimmerman, many Germans and natives surrendered to Spanish authorities, who then interned missionaries and others to Spain. Many natives in time actually returned to Kamerun. Still others found graves only God knows where.

One additional exploit remained for the Allies: Mora. In Kamerun's extreme north this mountainous stronghold had resisted both takeover and surrender for many months. General Cunliffe now sent its commander Officer von Raben an interesting proposition. If he and his people surrendered, the officers would be allowed to keep their swords, all Europeans would be sent to England as prisoners of war, and the native soldiers of the garrison would be given safe passage to their homes. Having been informed about Kamerun's surrender, Officer von Raben accepted General Cunliffe's offer. With the capitulation of Mora on February 19, 1916, the conquest of Kamerun was over, and Germany was dispossessed in due course of all its West African colonies.

By their march across the border to Spanish Rio Muni and by the surrender of Mora, thousands of colonial Kamerunians became homeless but at least safe from further Allied military pursuit and plunder. Only a few indomitable missionaries intent on shepherding their people and churches as long as possible managed to avoid or elude capture and imprisonment for a while.

At first, British prisons, especially those in London, were the major places of final incarceration for prisoners shipped from Duala. With movement to Spanish Rio Muni, however, exiled Kamerunians were now sent additionally to Spain, Fernando Po, Dahomey, and France.

Lessening munitions supplies finally convinced Governor Ebermeier to leave Kamerun whatever the cost, and although still legally subject to imprisonment, to head with his people for safety on foreign shores. They would be free to return to Kamerun after several years. In fact anyone, including soldiers, who wanted to leave before beginning or completing the anticipated trek of escape was free to do so, and without censure. No one left.

December 30, 1915, the German forces left Jaunde; on January 1, 1916, the Allies took over the virtually empty city. With only four days' lead over their pursuing enemies, the Germans determined nonetheless to win the race for freedom. Lugging miscellaneous possessions and supplies, tribes and families marched in caravan order on all kinds of terrain. At nights they rested in the bush on gathered branches. Many, especially Europeans, became ill. Bandages as needed were washed for reuse; banana leaves sufficed if needed. To confuse the Allies the marchers changed assumed routes periodically. By marching along with his people in this potential fiasco, Governor Ebermeier himself lent encouragement.

The crossover arrival in Rio Muni began on February 6. Company by company with captains, 95 officers, 450 Europeans, 5,000 black soldiers, 400 white civilians, and about 40,000 natives reached their destination. This historic masterpiece of leadership and determination has to this day never lost its merited acclaim.

Meanwhile General Dobell in Kamerun reported to the London War Minister his inability to recommend a further "drive." The war in Kamerun was over but not assigned imprisonments in London, Fernando Po, Spain and France.

"Thank God that I could witness wonders of God's grace and supply of all personal needs. Never before has the reality of Christ's presence and the truth of His promises been so realised; again and again I experienced that all God's promises are *Yes* and *Amen* in Him and to His praise."

— Bender in a letter to friends

14
CHANGING OF MANY GUARDS

Kenneth Scott Latourette's comprehensive overview provides a tailor-made appraisal also for evaluating Kamerun's Baptist colonial era (1884–1914).

Christianity approached 1914, he notes, on a rising tide and with mounting momentum. It had surmounted adversaries that threatened its survival and also widened its global outreach. The dedication of its proponents and of its multiplying movements matched anything in Christian history and left its impress on more of global humanity than ever. By 1913, Latourette comments, missionaries were decoding ancient languages into writing, translating and publishing Bibles for mass distribution, establishing schools by the hundred, challenging the survival of slavery, and nurturing virile Christian communities.

Since his Kamerun arrival in 1899, Bender, by 1914, had participated in and was still contributing to all these aspects of mission work. In the extended Duala area, he worked among unreached tribes as well as with established churches. In Soppo among his earliest ministry fellows were Saker's Fernando Po, Victoria, and Duala compeers, Joseph Burnley and Joseph Wilson.

It was mission enthusiast Eduard Scheve in Germany

who first commissioned Bender to Africa. It was Scheve likewise who housed blacks from Kamerun in his home and underwrote their education. Among these was M'Bene who taught seminarians in both Duala and Soppo and was a respected Bender co-worker. It was Scheve's Berlin church, moreover, where Alfred Bell, nephew of King Bell, visited in response to a newspaper advertisement, was converted, baptized, and on return to Duala helped link disparate Baptist churches into united fellowship and work. It was also Alfred Bell who at Victoria welcomed America's first German Baptist missionary appointee, August Steffens, and persuaded him to move to Duala.

In three decades, a short period indeed, Kamerun's political, economic, religious, and increasingly civilizational development manifested a series of successive energizing forces. They were a troublesome mixture, however, of unknown/pre-planned, good/bad, ingrained/imposed, domestic/foreign influences that took turns, so to speak, as self-posted guards of status-quo or deviating situations that were subject to change either at will or by force. Pre-War Kamerun career missionaries like Bender were contracted or at least responsible to mission organizations, European government officials, local governing appointees, and even commercial benefactors. In this turmoil they nonetheless remained dedicated to God and his compelling call to teach, evangelize, and integrate converts into the Lord's family.

Mission sagas, including that of early Kamerun Baptists, reveal disagreements, dissensions, and even power struggles among workers, not to mention interdenominational disputes, resistance toward both government officialdom and legislation, and even secular wheeling and dealing. Perhaps largely excused, explained, or justified as marks of inexperience, naiveté, or even zealotry, such tensions, particularly intensified by native, let alone international warfare, and no less by paganism and false religions, spawned difficulties that required bold confrontation by missionaries and their co-workers. While today's mission enterprises are not totally devoid of such earlier stumbling blocks, they will have avoided some of them at least by the important practice of hindsight. Some present-day changes, even reversals in mission philosophy and practice, are probably the consequence of witnessing and learning from yesteryears' situations.

Fortunately some workers in pre-War times courageously recognized the need for changes in mission operations. Bender's program, for example, of including seminarians and trainees in preaching and leadership responsibilities during even their years of schooling paid good dividends. During the war-imposed absence of white missionaries, insightful, well-trained blacks could therefore step in effectively to nurture orphaned schools and churches. The remarkable increase of converts and churches in Soppo and other areas manifested God's hand of approval and blessing. This development proved to be an important move toward native decision-making and independency.

One might say that almost the last in a series of inherited or installed mission perturbing phases had been met. Early ministry hurdles had moved from tribal confrontation to trial and error work situations, to mission society supervision, to European regulation, to international intrusion, to snippets of independence, and finally to self-defined freedom. So-called pioneer missionaries were present at and or part of these progressions. They no less than their God-entrusted African charges grew and matured with changing conditions and expectations. Only with spiritual faith, wisdom and dedication would endurance and hope prevail to realize the reality and joys of God's unalloyed presence and power.

By the fall of 1914 most Baptist and Basel and other mission workers (except perhaps the American Presbyterians) had left Kamerun as prisoners of war or were being held for later internment. Mission stations were plundered and left to enemy disposition. Most churches were small. Many members fled to the bush with their families. Schools were closed. The blacks' not uncommon fatalism and superstition, together with seeming resignation to "que sera sera" attitudes, countered the Christian emphasis on staying the course by word and life.

On the other hand the months of the battle-heavy and physically draining march from Jaunde to Rio Muni proved what proper motivation, good leadership, and joint endeavor under God could do. For many Kamerunians the only home they now had was the voluntary army on its line of march. For women slavery or death would be the only alternatives. As months of trekking during the rainy season, of gathering food, fighting skirmishes, and succumbing to illness or even death engulfed the would-be fugitives, they outfoxed their pursuers by negotiating their own choice of imprisonment under friendlier conditions.

The few missionaries still active in Kamerun ministry including the Benders were surely aware of the Allies' Jaunde setback. At the time they were also alert to and constructively involved in the Paris Evangelical Mission Society's efforts to restore and oversee school and church operations before what became mandate status for both parts of Kamerun. Five-sixths of the colony had been turned over to France and the remaining sliver to Britain. French became the official language in French Cameroun, and English was allowed in the British sector, which was now administered from Nigeria. Difficulties in ascertaining French and British boundaries and in trying to gain expected United States consent to the League of Nations mandate programs were actually not settled until July 20, 1922. France's final extensive booty included the port city Duala and its extended area that Britain had occupied from 1914 to 1916, the Cameroon River estuary, and the country's two railroads, all of which together enabled link-up with France's central African possessions. In addition the extensive piece of French Equatorial Territory that France had traded to Kamerun in 1911 in exchange for Germany's base in Morocco was returned to it. Britain's prize embraced the Nigerian border area of plantations, former capital Buea, and port city Victoria.

The ongoing unraveling and implementing of Versailles and other negotiations is still today a live topic for researchers and writers even among African scholars. Missions and missionaries of that era were especially concerned about other matters as well, however. First and foremost was their apprehension about war-victimized natives, their still-captive fellow missionaries, distant relatives including their children, and war-deserted properties. Fortunately, Allied governments ventured positive action about loss of properties. They agreed to turn over such stations, but only to French or British trustees or boards religiously or denominationally sympathetic to original mission founders or administrators such as the Baselers and the Baptists.

With its eighty-nine missionaries and over 13,000 native church members, Basel was the largest mission group in Kamerun before the War. When in 1886 Britain's protectorate, Victoria, yielded to Germany's Kamerun colonization, the German-Swiss Lutheran Basel Mission Society took over Alfred Saker's Victoria English Baptists.

As theological and/or synodical problems arose, however, many of the now Basel-related Baptists threw off this imposed identity, declared themselves totally independent, and moved to the Duala area. For all that, the work of Basel Mission so flourished in Kamerun that already before the War it had become the colony's largest Protestant group. Basel Mission was no inexperienced group, of course; it had settled elsewhere in Africa already in 1815. In relation to the German Baptists in Kamerun, however, it through the years for various reasons harbored an on and off ambivalent relationship; actually such feeling was not one-sided. Nonetheless both groups shared similar work goals and on occasion supported each other in times of mission stress and distress.

Part of the Paris Evangelical Mission Society's responsibilities included observing various missions' activities and also their attitudes toward governing policies. Maintenance of so-called neutrality during wartime was no easy matter; occasional political missteps or unfortunate comments could easily incur warnings or penalties. All in all, however, the individual ministries of Bergeret, Allegret, and Aymerich proved positive, helpful, and significant in their assigned locations and became as a group a kind of substitute authority in a time of nongovernorship or rulership.

As an American citizen and the only missionary permitted to remain in Kamerun throughout and even beyond the War, Bender met especially with Pastors Allegret and Bergeret. It was they who engineered the reopening of schools, for example, and who assisted black teachers and supervisors to define and practice their duties. Restoration of relative peace and order encouraged natives-in-hiding to return to their villages and many escapees to Rio Muni and beyond to re-enter Kamerun.

The Benders' practicalities for daily survival depended largely on their own Soppo compound maintenance, like restoring their soldier-destroyed garden, and on Hedwig's cookery and other domestic creativity. Substituting starchy native potatos and ground corn for flour, palm oil for shortening, and dried bananas for sugar or sweetening were relatively easy. Frequent meals of African palm chop were another resource. Not until cancelled shipping between New York and Europe to Kamerun was lifted were Western goods available, and that for a price. But with the War's cutoff of Berlin's Baptist Missionary Society financial support and inaccessibility of American funds as well, money became a missing commodity.

Under such circumstances, most helpful through the entire War and beyond were the ongoing visits of British seamen who deliberately planned stopovers with the Benders. Already from the time of the Benders' 1909 Soppo arrival the men had experienced a warm reception and genuine spiritual concern at the missionaries' home. There older navy personnel, as well as younger sometimes rather rootless sailors shared Bible readings, hymns, and prayers reminiscent perhaps of their British heritage but now possibly neglected or even forgotten. Bender once computed the number of such visits as about 300 over the years. Most rewarding, of course, were actual conversions to Christ in this subsidiary mission field.

The gifts of food or other items which often accompanied these men were a reminder, as it were, of God's feeding of Elijah by ravens (I Kings 17:4–6). As already indicated, unavailability of food in a time of uncertain overseas transport, and lack of money were ongoing problems. The Benders were therefore thrust as never before upon God and his promised care, and upon the practice of hospitality as their only negotiable human virtue.

Bender's well-kept ledger of assets and debits from 1914 through 1919 testifies to God's presence and oversight, and no less to his human agencies of concern and caring. Among the 1914 entries of ten named benefactors and their gifts are, for example, flour from British Major Rose; food from Basel Missionary Lutz; a leg of lamb roast from now friendly soldier McDougal; a hat by a Duala Provost Marshal; two bags of potatoes from Buea farmer Streetz; and eggs from Duala sergeant Dukelow. Among gifts from again ten donors in 1915 were two caps from Captain Demwood; three months' prepaid milk by McDougal; an art kit by Mr. Boniface; a fruit cake by Missionary Cooper; and four loads of fertilizer from Captain Spencer. In 1916 gifts from among seven donors were a pound of tea and two boxes of sugar from Dr. Unwin; assorted foodstuffs from Mr. Adams of Her Majesty's vessel "Highfly"; and food from Bender's trainee now Duala pastor Lotin Same. In 1917 nine donors' gifts included quinine from Dr. Moreland; fabric from Missionary Cooper; and a pair of shoes from a sailor of Her Majesty's vessel "Astraea." Among 1918's entries are a dress and a doll for now three-year-old daughter Helga from Mrs. Gardiner; stockings from an "Astraea" sailor; food from Paris Missionary Society Bergeret; one chicken from Soppo substation Wolifamba; ten pounds of coffee and packets of dried fish from Mr. Mueller; and four cans of cheese from Monsignor De Coninck.

The final year of 1919 included food once again from missionary Bergeret; an enormous supply of food from "Astraea" sailors; then in Rotterdam, the Netherlands,

expected point of departure for the United States, together
with a gift from someone at the Hague, almost 500 German
marks' worth of assorted supplies. The ledger entries from
1920 until the Benders' 1929 through 1935 resumed
ministry are equally interesting and in some respects quite
revealing.

Under the War's strictures of missionary
imprisonments, loss of normal government, imposition of
foreign controls, not to mention military carnage and
devastation, the Benders' ministries concentrated largely
on readying natives for perhaps soon takeover of
leadership. Despite problems of maintaining school
attendance because of war complexities or incitements
Bender stressed besides biblical study the learning and
practicing of self-discipline and independence as essential
for ministry. Continuing his method of taking trainees
with him on trips for station visitation, he himself
demonstrated and then assigned to his students
opportunities to emulate ways and means of evangelism,
instruction, and discipling. Granted that practice of these
concepts has today too often been refined simply to a
special art, Bender's exercise of valid compassion and
burden for lost souls and growing believers was primarily
Spirit-born and Spirit-driven. In his seminarians he hoped
to see develop and mature this kind of God-given mind
and prayer set that he himself needed and sought to
model.

The reality of Kamerun's official geographical and
supervisory division in 1916 affected not only what was
left of the now absent missionaries' work but also that of
their African replacements. The five-sixths of the colony
entrusted to France spelled "Cameroun" and the
remaining one-sixth sliver allotted to Britain spelled

"Cameroon" became a unique composite of different powers and cultures that historically had not necessarily been the cosiest of bedfellows. The fact that the Kamerunians were not consulted in this division, one determined not on linguistic or ethnic but purely on geographical lines, created problems that remained for over forty years.

France assumed that its share of West African subjects would in time become French citizens and accordingly established a pyramid type of rulership geared to that end. At the top was the Minister of Colonies, a member of the distant Paris hierarchy. Under him was the Dakar-located Governor General of West Africa. Under him were separate governors of individual West African colonies. Authoritarian in character this pyramid system involved little thought, however, about ground-level governing of vanquished tribal people. French Cameroun therefore became simply another unit of France's larger colonial regime.

British Cameroon, on the other hand, during this same upcoming mandate period, came under the direction of Lord Frederick Lugard and his system of Indirect Rule. Born in India the son of a British regiment chaplain there, Lugard spent most of his years unraveling problems in Britain's sub-Saharan colonies. Nigeria where he stayed until 1919 became the last of such assignments. As a leading member of the League of Nations mandate committee he understood the purposes and ramifications of colonial administration and superintendence. Although not signed by the League until July 20, 1922, mandates had been projected years earlier. Their aim was to promote the material, moral well-being, and social progress of the mandates' inhabitants. Responsible for checking their operation at close range were people like Lugard. The system consisted largely of selected community chiefs or elders who together with various councils of their own people were responsible for determining and implementing local matters like sanitation, health care, roads, taxes, and so on. The basic idea was to exercise liberty and self-development of such a kind that everyone's interests and religion as well were safe. The best way to secure such self-development was to allow natives freedom to manage their own affairs through their own chiefs or elders but under the guidance and eye of British staff.

This kind of power decentralization to develop coordinating authority was perceived in part as a stepping stone to future independence. That realization, of course, would depend on the quality and integrity of its participants. Critics of Indirect Rule viewed it therefore as an uncertain commodity for governing and probably even a hindrance to genuine progress. These governmental changes from German to post-War progressive efforts were yet another of Bender's many missionary experiences. On various occasions he consulted personally or by letter with Lugard about mission affairs. Since British Cameroon bordered on Nigeria, and parts of it were actually in Nigeria, Lagos was its as well as Governor General Lugard's capital city and headquarters.

It was their American citizenship and their Christian conviction to do so that enabled the Benders to remain in Kamerun without a break from 1914 to 1919. Those extended years had taken them from the peaceful launching in 1914 of the first promising interdenominational mission conference to and through the devastations of an intertribal, interracial, international, intercontinental, and interreligious war. Thrust from all sides into maintaining their equilibrium in the midst of constant upheaval, and ministering as God's servants and representatives whatever and wherever the need might be was their daily portion of courageous engagement. As missionaries they were not, as someone has observed, "spiritual robots functioning in a tightly controlled Magic Kingdom ... where things seldom go awry."

The Benders had seen missionary co-workers abused, interned, and imprisoned, natives misled and deceived, personal possessions pilfered, and properties demolished. They had seen abandoned corpses, distraught widows, and fatherless children. Their own children in Europe were beyond reach. Apart from assurance of divine help, endurance, and hope the Benders would surely have despaired.

Their divine work assignment disallowed despair, however. It called, rather, for exercising and modeling faith in God's ordering and working all things for good to his glory. And that surely was the case as natives recognized their need of spiritual answers to their earthly plights. Nationwide including Soppo, hundreds now thronged to churches as never before, laying a foundation for post-war Christian progress. Teaching and preaching trainees rallied to take over ministries. With missionaries' help visions grew once again for cooperative even interdenominational assemblies. Groups like the United Baptists of Cameroon or the European Baptist Mission with native pastors came into being as a portent of perhaps in time an International Baptist Mission or even an Interdenominational Fellowship or Partnership. Paris Evangelical Mission appointee Pastor Allegret showed special wisdom in motivating this kind of interchurch and interdenominational development.

For the Benders the time had therefore come to retire. Many of their trainees had become pastors of churches, the Paris Mission was functioning effectively, and aspects of governmental development were in place in both the French and British sectors. All that remained for them to implement was official ordination of someone as pastor of Soppo station. That person was well-trained and well-experienced Laban Moki. To him Bender entrusted preaching, teaching, and pastoral responsibilities. To him Bender also turned over occupancy of the missionaries' residence.

Goodbyes were said with assurance of God's timing and of his approval of Laban Moki's entrusted leadership. Would white missionaries ever return to post-War Kamerun? If so, who and when?

Carl Bender and
Trained Cameroon Workers

15
GOING HOME 1919

Carl and Hedwig Bender had not had a furlough since 1913, at which time in Germany they had taken a family picture of their five children and themselves. Now in 1919 a sixth child, daughter Helga born in 1915, joined the ranks, so to speak, to meet her siblings for the first time, who, similarly for their first time, could meet and see her. Because of the War's interrupted and highly censored, sometimes destroyed postal deliveries they may not even have known about her existence for some time. One thing that would have impressed them, of course, was the fact that Helga had had the privilege of remaining with her parents rather than being brought to Berlin as they had been. Herbert, the eldest, was now fifteen when he and Helga, almost five, first met. All the eight Benders, of course, would face the challenge of joining hands and especially hearts in the years ahead.

Sailing from Victoria—with Helga entertaining passengers with African songs—the Benders arrived in Liverpool, England, on November 12, 1919. From here they continued to London where Bender negotiated travel and legal affairs before continuing to Berlin and the nearby Neuruppin Missionaries' Children's Home. Saying farewell to their friends, loving deaconesses, school masters, and others whom they would probably never see again was not easy for the older Bender children. Neither was the prospect easy of learning to become a united family and doing so, moreover, in an unknown country and environment.

Their train travel from Berlin to Zürich in neutral Switzerland and on to seaport Rotterdam in neutral Netherlands brought them to the sailing date for New York. With reservations in hand, Bender nonetheless had strange misgivings about sailing as scheduled. He therefore cancelled his trip for later departure on the next vessel. During the interim of waiting he preached in several Kamerun-supporting Dutch churches, conveyed up-to-date information about Soppo's now British Cameroon situation, and for himself caught up on world post-War developments.

One morning Bender heard the shocking news that the ship whose reservations he had cancelled had on its trip to New York struck an iceberg and sunk with great loss of life. Once again for him and Hedwig and perhaps for the first time for their children, God reconfirmed his care of them and his assurance of yet unknown but nonetheless trust-enforcing futures. The Benders would later learn, moreover, that the ship following their actual Rotterdam departure had also struck an iceberg.

Like many immigrants of that day Benders travelled steerage "class" to the United States at ten dollars per person. The word "class" was and still is really a misnomer. In earlier times slaves and cattle had crowded the space below portholes now reserved for crowds of clear-minded and hardiness-inspected bodies. Because of pioneer years in Africa the senior Benders adjusted more easily to steerage conditions than did their Berlin-oriented and pre-college-curriculum-educated children. Ongoing evidence of seasickness everywhere and at all times on board ship was difficult to handle in view of the unavailability of privacy. Son Herbert's calls for a "receptacle" became routine and were long jokingly remembered by the family. Doors marked "Closed" failed to open despite the word's suggestion of the German word "Kloset"(toilet). For Helga the worst ordeal of all was examination for head lice. The persistence of three aggressive doctors prevailed, however, and probably established her life-long indisposition to medical attention.

The important thing, of course, was safe arrival at Ellis Island. Because the missionaries Bender had on their 1908 furlough trip already met United States entry clearance requirements, they were now spared many of the tedious Ellis Island procedures and soon on a train heading from New York City to Buffalo, New York. The arrival date was February 12, 1920. Carl Ronald Bender insisted that the colorful and elaborate decorations everywhere were in honor of his tenth birthday!

Home again! What did, what would that really mean? After an absence of twenty years since Carl Bender's original 1899 departure, at what point and how would his reinstatement to original family begin? While age and frailty had overtaken his parents they were at least still alive to welcome not only their son, once earmarked for inevitable demise in Africa, but also six stalwart grandchildren and their lovely mother. (They gave to each a Hershey's candy bar.) Fortunately German language fluency and reasonably good English guaranteed ready and steady streams of conversation not only with grandparents, but also with three aunts, an uncle, and increasing numbers of other people.

Visits to Buffalo High Street and to Third Baptist churches were soon made, of course, to thank faithful supporters of the Cameroon work and to orient the Bender children to attendance and participation in American churches. Of quick concern was also registration at public schools, not to mention finding simple housing.

Across wide fields behind the house they found on Stockbridge Avenue at the edge of town in an undeveloped subdivision, a new school had recently opened and before long it absorbed the six Bender children. Thorwald was assigned to transport Helga on his bicycle handlebars to and from kindergarten; he and the other siblings walked to learn under five different teachers in five different grades.

Meanwhile, contributions of army cots and other basic furniture, as well as of food, found their way to the Benders' little house. The four boys bunked in the cold unfinished attic, the women and Carl Bender shared sleeping quarters downstairs. Sitting on front porch steps at early twilight after a day's varied involvements became a frequent means of meeting neighbors and of sharing in area activities.

Was this program of settlement beginning to define the concept of home for the transplanted Berlin children and for their American-by-marriage mother Hedwig Bender? Of this missionary family, only Carl Bender had now returned to an authentic established home of his memory. Would his children somewhere, somehow, find or themselves create such a home to eclipse the deprivation of earlier years? Would Hedwig Bender ever be truly at home in America?

What, in fact, is home? For missionaries who passionately identify themselves with their fields of service, for missionaries' children who vacillate between service, for missionaries' children who vacillate between dual or multiple loyalties, where and what is home? How or why for retired missionaries is the abiding compulsion to return to their field of labor a yearning for home?

During this period of adjustment, perhaps especially for his family, Carl Bender spent almost a year for the North American Baptists in promoting and gathering funds for former Kamerun. His ledger records gifts from identified persons or churches in Connecticut, Florida, Iowa, Kansas, Michigan, Minnesota, North Dakota, New York, Ohio, and Canada. Prominent sources of support were four Buffalo churches and the Newark, New Jersey Baptist Church where his brother-in-law, his sister Helen's husband Henry Schroeder, was pastor. He included a visit, of course, to Rochester German Baptist Seminary where alumnus August Steffens, first American German Baptist appointee to Kamerun, had studied, as well as close friend and co-worker Valentin Wolff, who with his family in time settled and pastored like the Benders in the Lebanon/Watertown, Wisconsin, area. How car-less Bender negotiated all his travels is not recorded. In his mission development assignments local or nearby situations were, as in Africa, just a long trek-cum-cane away. His mission receipts for 1920-1921 until his move to Watertown totalled $1,481.27, not an insignificant sum in those days.

Alongside raising money for the denomination's missions program, Bender, between 1919 and 1932, gathered separate private funds to help support his revered Soppo evangelists. This he did by securing a total of eight individuals, Sunday school classes, and women's societies to "adopt" these workers. Joseph Burnley received $200; Laban Moki, $225; Briggs and Embola, $75 each; Meende, Efeme, and Ekuta, $50 each; and Efase, $40. These donors were from Philadelphia, Buffalo, Chicago, and Lebanon, Wisconsin.

Bender's third project involved providing and shipping at his own expense pencils, paper, notebooks, and sermons and teaching materials prepared by him in the Duala language. Most appreciated probably were Bender's regular letters of encouragement and sometimes advice in regard to their expressed needs and/or problems.

The Benders' time of going home obviously became for their children a significant initiation into the realities of missionaries' family life and vocational calling, and for Carl and Hedwig a reminder of missionaries' non-retirement from a plethora of ministry opportunities.

16

WATERTOWN 1921–1925

The Benders' choice of Watertown as the best of three pastoral opportunities depended first of all on prayer confirmation. Seeking God's will for each day let alone for the chapters of a lifetime had been an ingrained discipline and practice throughout Carl's and Hedwig's marriage, and was being learned now as well by their children.

One factor in opting for Watertown was its small size as compared to the bigness of the other cities. The year in Buffalo had started family bonding in a constructive way. Now the time had come to develop community bonding that nurtured opportunity and individual freedom, growth, and independence among and along with friendly and supportive fellow citizens. Watertown seemed right for such a lifestyle.

New Englanders pushing westward were among the earliest Watertown settlers. Most numerous, however, were German immigrants who promptly developed farms, built homes, and established essential businesses. By the 1850s Watertown had become the state's second largest city and together with Milwaukee and Madison counted on the triple railroad system being constructed for additional progress and success. When its undergirding $400,000 financing collapsed, however, so did

Watertown's hopes for continued strength; the city, in fact, slumped to its earlier limits and limitations.

On April 20, 1921, having occupied four rows of seats and eaten a generous supply of homemade lunch, the eight Benders arrived by train in this town of Watertown. Meeting them with Model T Fords were the Karbergs of Pipersville, a rural hamlet several miles outside the city. Leading members of the First Baptist Church, they housed and fed the Benders in their farm home for several days while the parsonage (assuredly no manse) was readied for occupancy. The Karberg home, notwithstanding horsehair bed mattresses, oil lamps, outside water pumps, and outhouse plumbing, was often a place of accommodation and Christian fellowship. In his frequent visiting of members Bender looked forward to and enjoyed the five-mile walk, hat on head, cane in hand, to gather with Deacon Karberg and his family. Situated along the Rock River the Karberg farm on occasion also supplied a needed baptismal site.

First Baptist Church, the fifteenth church to be established in Watertown, was on Division Street, so named to mark the boundary between Dodge and Jefferson counties. Infrequent references in the church minutes of those early days to the parsonage at 214 Division Street seem to refer only to needed repairs. To the Benders, however, it became—architectural monstrosity or not—a center of spiritual development and a base for creative learning.

The front door led directly into the family living room. Here with its secondhand but serviceable furniture and cold linoleum floor, everyone gathered in the evening for Bible reading and to kneel for a whole round of family prayers. The pot-bellied stove was always either too far away or too close, although the room's small ceiling register allowed a wisp of heat to escape into Bender's upstairs study. The prized item in the living room was an excellent piano with a double bench where Erica and Herbert, trained in Germany, played fourhanded. Thorwald and Carl Ronald played violin. Armin also played piano in the early Watertown years, but acted primarily as "conductor of the family orchestra." Helga, taught by sister Erica, had just begun piano lessons. Frequently friends were invited for mini-concerts and in keeping with European tradition, listened quietly throughout without any talking.

To one side of the family living room was the "church living room"—sealed off by sliding doors and used only for weddings or for entertaining dignitaries. It boasted a wool rug, a settee, and several chairs.

The living room opened into the dining room. Here a long table always set with white linen tablecloth and napkins in personalized linen envelopes or napkin rings accommodated the eight Benders and two boarders. The latter helped supplement the parsonage income. One of the boarders was Marie Kupfer, a former deaconess in the Berlin Children's Home and therefore well known to the Bender children; she had come from Germany after the War and lived with the Benders while she worked in the local shoe factory. She and Helga shared an upstairs bedroom.

Adjoining the dining room was the kitchen where a door to the basement gave access to coal for the pot-bellied stove and wood for the kitchen stove. Here also Hedwig Bender's home-preserved fruits and vegetables were kept as well as large crocks of candled eggs. In the kitchen was the wood-hungry stove, with a compartment for heating water. The only kitchen furniture beside the stove was an old chair and a wooden table where twice a

week Hedwig baked whole wheat bread. Erica helped
with assorted kitchen chores. Thorwald kneaded the
bread.

Washing was a major operation. After being scrubbed
on a washboard stationed in a large wooden tub, the
laundry was boiled in a large copper tub atop the stove.
After rinsing, the clothes were wrung piece by piece
through a hand ringer, then hung outdoors to dry. Heavy
black irons heated and reheated on the stove were used for
pressing clothes on a flat, not folding ironing board.
Starching of Bender's shirt cuffs and separate shirt collars
were a part of weekly laundry.

On Wednesday night, April 27, 1921, Pastor Bender
presided at his first congregational business meeting. Its
agenda and discussion related first of all to financial
matters that Bender presented in his typically orderly way.

No. 1: The German Baptist Mission Board promised
to pay half of his not yet officially stated salary.

No. 2: Bender was returning the $11.81 balance left
from $185 allotted him for family train travel
from Buffalo.

No. 3: Toward cleaning and repairing the church
perhaps all members over eighteen years of age
could pay thirty-five cents, those younger,
fifteen cents.

(Many of his people, Bender knew, had little money
but they nonetheless sent modest gifts to German Baptists
working among post-War victims in Austria, Syria, and
the Middle East.)

No. 4: The church's wood-burning stove and lighting
system both needed costly repair.

(As an aside Bender reported he was glad to be

helping paint the inside of the church.)

At a later congregational meeting Bender joyfully reported the need of a baptismal service. Sons Thorwald and Carl Ronald had been converted, had passed the deacons' oral examination, and were ready for immersion baptism. Bender's years in Africa had prepared him well for outdoor river baptismal gatherings. Here in Watertown, Rock River near Karbergs' farm became First Baptist Church's baptistry.

Frequent missions or denominationally related visitors came to visit the Benders, sometimes to recall seminary or other past experiences, or to indicate the present state of affairs at mission and church headquarters. Such visits often took place in Bender's study away from household hubbub. On one such occasion a Wisconsin association representative of rotund frame stepped unthinkingly on Bender's floor register. Appearing downstairs to the amazed Bender children dangled a good-sized leg that definitely needed extraction.

While the Benders seldom experienced surprises of this order their days were never dull. Herbert, an ardent ecologist and defender of all things living, was often gifted on his desk at school with dead or squirming beasties. Thorwald attracted all manner of stray dogs or cats that he summarily brought home and hosted as long as possible. His dove cote in the church's old barn was always aflutter with arrivals or departures. Carl and Armin operated would-be telegraphy on wires strung between trees, or tried on terra firma as politely and apologetically as possible to retrieve misdirected footballs from an unhappy neighbor. In the playhouse Bender had made for her, Helga gathered friends for girlish make-believes, or she climbed to her very own tree bench to escape her brothers. Erica was more domestically involved except in summers when she swam like a fish from the East Main Street Bridge across the Rock River to the opposite shore.

During winter ice skating on the river or sleigh rides were orders of the day. One year's supreme achievement during heavy snows, however, was the building of a large round igloo. After hollowing it out for sitting inside around a real if small fire the boys daily maintained its outer frozen crust by dousing it with water. This is just one example of the Benders' innovative fun.

More important were school and school-related activities. All six children had their own study nooks with a small desk and chair next to their army-cot beds. Three of the boys were in one bedroom. Armin had a secondhand double bed in the upstairs open hall the slats of which kept collapsing. He had a very private "study," however, a long narrow passage under the eaves of the slanting roof and accessed by a door. There he sat on the floor and read to his heart's content. Helga's special spot—not really a study—was an old church pew in the hall outside the bathroom. Here people sat, waiting in line for their turn. But here, too, Helga propped her dolls.

Father's study, as indicated, was upstairs above the living room. His door was always closed and entrance was gained only by knocking for admittance. Once inside it was a wonderful place of filled bookshelves, a large roll top desk, and a chair or two. Pa, as they called him, really enjoyed helping the children with their homework, especially with written assignments. An excellent and experienced writer himself, he made suggestions and corrections if needed. As an artist he showed what progress he had made or hoped to make on a new canvas. Meantime, Ma downstairs at her sewing machine was restyling hand-me-down clothes, mending, or tackling a major project like sewing mattress covers for all eight beds, a task she completed on arrival at Watertown. Erica, besides keeping up with piano work, crocheted artful necklaces to sell.

Before finishing local schools and moving elsewhere most of the Bender children had odd jobs to earn pin money (allowances were non-existent) or even to contribute toward home expenses. Herbert dug graves in a local cemetery. Thorwald bought a cheap topless jalopy with poor brakes to sell Wearever Aluminum. Armin wrote and sold for ten cents a neighborhood news sheet and also had a paper route. Helga sold thread, pins and needles, and buttons from house to house, although much of her supply eventually went to Ma. Carl Ronald mowed lawns.

Saturdays had two fixed routines. One was a morning walk together by the younger Bender children to Watertown's Carnegie Library to exchange the past week's books for a new stack of reading. With this accomplished the entire family, as weather permitted, then marched two by two to Riverside Park for a picnic lunch and perhaps some boating or other activity. The remainder of the day was given to checking out the church for Sunday readiness and for checking out oneself as to clothes and polishing shoes. Pa Bender did the ladies' slippers and lined them up at their bedroom doors. In the kitchen potatoes were peeled for Sunday cooking, and other vegetables were prepared as well. Meat and baked goods required only Sunday heating or freshening.

After the rigors and many activities of the work week Sunday hours were safeguarded as much as possible for worship and quiet renewal of body and soul. Except obviously for Pastor Bender, the rest of the family all sat together in the same row every week and in the same pew.

Doing so made a statement of familial and generational unity and harmony in the Lord and in his name.

In its annual September organizational meeting the church in 1921 approved having special evangelistic meetings in the near future. Sunday evening services, moreover, were to be in English on a three-month trial basis. As for practical matters, double windows were requisitioned for the cold north side of the parsonage, and also apparatus for supplying hot water in the kitchen and in the bathroom. To help navigate traffic in the latter, which had been installed after their arrival from Buffalo, Mrs. Bender had sewn heavy draperies to divide the almost nine by twelve area into three parts, thus making all of them individually and simultaneously accessible. This homemade technological feat lessened the Benders' use of the church's grape-arbor hidden outhouse a short walk from both church and parsonage. Yes, things were indeed on the move.

What's more, the pastor's annual salary of $100 a month was increased an extra $100 for the year, though its payment in part with farm produce or staples would continue as before. In this, as in the years reminiscent of Soppo, the Benders similarly recalled the sailors' and others' life-sustaining food contributions to them in war-time Africa. God's wherevers and whenevers of meeting all needs as he promised still evoked thankful "yeas" and "amens."

The Benders' entire family, until some of them left Watertown, participated in First Baptist Church activities. Already in 1922 Erica was one of two morning organists and Herbert, one of two evening and midweek appointees. Others took care of heating the church—bringing in the wood, lighting the fire, stoking it, and removing the ashes. Mother Bender's practical nursing and deaconess experience kept her busy among city folk as well as church members. Her prompt and successful attention to burn victims across the street, for example, became a frequent topic of neighborhood conversations. Her expert hot and/or cold wraps were standard treatment for most Bender ailments, infrequent as they were, and for her own severe migraine headaches as well.

Pastoral visitation by her alone or with her husband was not only expected but practiced voluntarily. She also fed freight car hoboes of those days whose fence post or other markings identified for each other where to get a good meal as well as conversation with the man of the house. Regularly after Sunday evening services the Benders joined forces to entertain whole or parts of families as a means of getting to know them in depth. Hedwig prepared the coffee and simple snacks, Pastor Carl cleared the table and washed the dishes.

The Benders seldom practiced preachers' traditional "Mondays off." Among other things, always waiting upstairs in the roll top desk were projected article or sermon outlines to develop and memos for letters to write, especially those to Benders' Soppo workers. On their behalf Bender wrote letters also to American churches and individuals for mission contributions. He also sought mission speakers for the Watertown church and on occasion he himself visited other churches as a mission speaker or representative.

Another regular task for Bender, one that was self-imposed to help understand and appreciate his people, was maintaining his gifts and debits ledger. During the first full year in Watertown fifty people had contributed money or goods—mostly food—worth $395 as appraised by Bender or about $75 worth per month. The names of the donors of both large and small gifts told their own stories. The size and nature of the gifts, frequency of giving, and other considerations could be an index to congregational composition and character. The reticent widow's humble gift could spiritually outclass the pretentious rich man's gold.

As the Benders received contributions of food and used it, there must have been reflections occasionally on the who, what, why, and so on of their benefactors. Would they enjoy Benders' simple meals?   Breakfast included cooked oatmeal or cream of wheat, homemade whole wheat bread and margarine, homemade jam or sometimes honey, and sometimes an egg. On school days the children came home for a lunch of homemade soup, such as lentil, and a sandwich. The day's major meal was at night. Meat was served only three times a week. Vegetables of all kinds were the backbone of the Benders' cuisine, and were often harvested from the pastor's own large garden that he tended in early, pre-breakfast hours. Framing the vegetable garden on all four sides were colorful flowers that bloomed at various but interlocking times.

Bender had no aspirations whatever to be "a big name." His relationships were always straightforward, and he met people with a pleasant smile. He walked almost everywhere with his ivory-handled ebony cane, not because of physical necessity but as a side by side tapping companion. In Africa, of course, he always carried a stick or cane to help manage difficult physical terrain or if necessary, to ward off troublesome creatures. Here in America the cane was a happy reminder of Soppo, a memory that he always hoped might be enlarged by a return there, God willing and God enabling. Whether in "the Study" or on the streets, he meditated with and about God, organizing articles, outlining sermons, and planning helps for his Soppo as well as for his Watertown people. For Missionary Bender the Watertown years provided a congregation within a congregation, namely his children. Watertown offered opportunity to overcome the experience of their necessary separation years in Berlin by so displaying God's work of grace in the church community, that family members would similarly grow in spiritual commitment. The ten-year disparity between Herbert, now sixteen, and Helga, six, was never a problem as one might have expected. The orderly training and educational discipline absorbed in Germany among the Children's Home's diverse constituency, together with the joy and privilege of now being a united family at a new frontier of experience formulated a wholesome atmosphere of mutuality without hindering creative independency.

By 1925 when Bender's Watertown ministry ended, each of the children was evidencing interests or abilities that would climax in later professions. Thorwald, having left home to study in Chicago, would become pastor of both American Baptist and North American Baptist churches and also professor of theology in their separate seminaries. His early student pastorate, interestingly, was the Lebanon, Wisconsin, Baptist Church which years earlier in the 1880s had helped found the Watertown German Baptist Church. Erica, also in Chicago, pursued nurse's training at West Suburban Hospital and was graduated "as most likely to succeed." She was also an adjunct in piano at the Chicago School of Music. Armin, at Ravenswood High School in Chicago, a promising writer of both prose and poetry, received a poetry scholarship to the University of Rochester, New York. There, during his freshman year, he lived in the same dormitory that his father had occupied years ago during seminary. During that year the University divested itself of its long-time Baptist background and seminary connections. The seminary divided into two parts, as it were— independent Colgate-Rochester Divinity School, and independent North American Baptist Seminary of Sioux Falls, South Dakota. Armin's literary expertise and acumen opened a teaching role for him at the University but especially his appointment as President Valentine's assistant and speech writer. Carl Ronald, also a Chicago Ravenswood High School honor graduate, who practiced his valedictory speech in the Gross Park Immanuel Baptist Church auditorium, studied architecture at the University of Illinois. There he received a graduate scholarship to Italy but lacked additional funds to accept it, even as Armin had to forego a Rhodes scholarship to England. Herbert, the linguist, fluent in German, French, and English from the years in Germany and later to add several other languages as well, received a scholarship in Watertown to the University of Wisconsin at Madison, known in those years as radically socialist. After two years he fled that scene for New York City where he completed his studies and secured work at Chase National Bank. In due course he was invited to help establish a branch in Shanghai, China, but refused the offer, preferring to remain in New York, a city he loved passionately and where he spent the rest of his life.

Helga's life has been no less interesting. Born in Africa during the War she was therefore not transferable, so to speak, to Berlin to join her siblings. She remained in Africa with her parents until 1919, and as already indicated, did not meet her brothers and sister until the family gathered for their trip from Rotterdam to New York for life in the United States. She was the only one of the Benders ever to be hospitalized during the Watertown years. In February, 1924, at the Douglas elementary school playground, she and other students were trying out the new ten-foot high steel slide. Standing at the top and about to sit down she somehow misstepped and striking all the metal supports on the way, fell head first to the ground. Rushed to then St. Mary's Hospital with a double skull fracture and bleeding profusely, she lay unconscious for two weeks. Day and night her parents took turns at her bedside, bringing all the food for their vigils. If and when she opened her eyes, they reasoned, she ought to see a familiar face rather than have the shock of facing a stranger. Neighbors and friends stopped by to add their prayers. Some brought fruit, others brought new clothing in expectation of Helga's recovery. Hospital staff and doctors were surprised when she regained consciousness. She did, however, but had lost the ability to walk. Confined to the parsonage for the rest of the school year, she managed to keep up with studies sufficiently to be promoted. As for the walking problem, Carl Ronald faithfully worked with her every day until she regained mobility; he became, and rightly so, especially dear to her among the four brothers. Years later when Carl Ronald contracted fatal leukemia, perhaps related to Agent Orange exposure in World War II, Helga flew to his hospital bedside in Chicago where he had died just minutes earlier, and rode with his body to the mortuary. She knew he was with the Lord. Both he and Armin were with navy intelligence in the Pacific arena, Carl Ronald with mapping to identify hits and strikes, Armin, with logistical reporting and news briefs. Carl had also shared in architecturally setting up one of the military bases.

Like her brothers Helga attended Ravenswood High

School in Chicago but only for three years; she returned to Watertown for the senior year, finished as salutatorian, and was offered a scholarship to Carroll College. She opted to attend Wheaton College, however, and worked her way through by helping in the German and French departments. There she also met Carl F. H. Henry, with whom she has shared more than a half-century of challenging ministries overseas and in America. She eventually earned two master's degrees, became a dean of women in a state teachers' college, became an associate professor of education, taught at two seminaries, and with Carl assisted with teaching and lectures in various Asian countries, Australia, and Europe. She had even been a seminary librarian to get her P. H. T. (Putting Hubby Through)! She also wrote several books and numerous articles. One reason for here including this detailed post-Watertown picture of the Bender children is to indicate that "MKs" (Missionaries' Kids), however unusual and even unfortuitous their lives may be or become, can and do "make the grade" with God's patient help, and can be a witness to the faith of their missionary parents, who must yield their children in special ways to divine governance and safekeeping. Missionary life is not for sissies—nor is MK life.

Church growth at First Baptist Church in Watertown was slow. There were converts and new members from time to time, to be sure, and an occasional new immigrant from Germany. But it was a slow process for one whose original vision of ministry had been the conversion of perhaps hundreds if not thousands in Africa. Bender carried a heavy burden in Watertown. Some members moved to full-time English-speaking and affiliated churches in the area; others moved for better work opportunities. As the poor, the sick, and the elderly fell behind with pledges, church committees shifted book balances from one fund to another. Finances actually always seemed to be a problem. Yet attendance did show gains, and more space was needed, especially for Sunday school work and activities. Bender continued to work indefatigably, spending hours in prayer and sermon preparation and in pastoral visitation. He never owned a car, but as on the mission field he liked to walk and to converse with people along the way. On occasion he even walked to minister to a needy church member who lived ten miles from the church.

Perhaps it came as a surprise and perhaps it did not, when on Sunday, July 5, 1925, Bender announced that he had received a call from Gross Park Immanuel Baptist Church in Chicago. He hoped, he added, to take up this new work in August. He met promptly with Watertown church committees to discuss ways of enlarging their Sunday school facilities, but spoke also about perhaps seeking new church properties. He proposed building a new church, and, in fact, helped sketch a structure that anticipated the edifice that in time materialized at South Fifth and Dodge streets where the church remained almost sixty years before moving to its present location overlooking Highway 16. In moving to its present location the church left behind its cornerstone in the Fifth Street property bought by the Apostolic Gospel Lighthouse. The cornerstone presumably contains historical papers and artifacts bearing on the Baptist church's beginnings. Left in place also are lovely stained glass windows commemorating the lives of some of Watertown's Baptist pioneers and leaders.

Immanuel Baptist Church in Chicago meanwhile

requested membership release letters for Carl J. and Hedwig Bender, for daughter Erica, and sons Carl Ronald and Armin. Helga was not yet a church member, and Thorwald and Herbert were already members out-of-state. The Bender family as a unit was beginning to face separation once again, but now for different reasons than those of the earlier years in Africa.

17
CHICAGO 1925–1929–1932

The years 1925 to 1929, when Bender pastored the Gross Park Immanuel Baptist Church at Damen and Newport Avenues in Chicago, were more significant as an interim transition to the restoration of long-interrupted missionary work in Cameroon than for suburban evangelism. To be sure, Immanuel Baptist Church was already energetically engaged in community outreach. It was three times the size of the Watertown congregation and instead of a constituency in those days composed largely of farmers, Immanuel was comprised mostly of upper middle-class office workers with significant participation also by teachers and nurses. The Chicago metropolitan area offered interaction with other North American Baptist leaders and church members that kept alive the denomination's missionary interests. Immanuel was important as a central Midwest location for North American German Baptists, and it was within the orbit of North American Baptist headquarters located in the suburban Chicago community of Forest Park.

Immanuel Church was a transition point for Mission Board leaders and workers, not a few of whom were entertained or lodged on occasion in the church parsonage at 1947 Newport Avenue. The leadership of Dr. William

Kuhn as head of the Home Mission Board played a major role in maintaining communication with the Berliner Missions Gesellschaft (Berlin Missions Society) and in helping formulate the needed transition of the North American German Baptist Missions Society to assume and control future missionary reengagement in Cameroon. Few subjects were more often on the minds and in the hearts of denominational workers than the fate of missionary endeavor in Cameroon, where the British had evicted missionary personnel and imprisoned others who, like Valentin and Helene Wolff, had refused to sign papers attesting that the missionaries were well treated by British forces, and who therefore declined to gloss over War atrocities they had seen as the price of their freedom. Bender's singular ministry as an American in Africa placed him in new ways at a strategic center of these discussions, and the urgent plea of denominational leaders that he return to Africa in 1929 came at the climax of his ministry at Immanuel.

When the Benders arrived in Chicago by train from Watertown, the family numbered five—the parents, Carl Ronald, Armin, and Helga. Thorwald and Erica were already ensconced in Chicago, engaged in both work and study, although they now also began attending Immanuel. Arriving in tandem from Watertown with the Benders was Missionary Bender's well-used library and the most expensive possession that the family had acquired in Wisconsin, a quality upright piano.

Baptist business meetings, if they are at all alive, are notorious for spirited disagreements on secondary matters. Immanuel was no exception. One wit remarked that Baptists need to sponsor annual revival meetings to overcome the spiritual losses of their quarterly business sessions. The minutes at Immanuel seem not to illumine the issue, and there is no reason to believe that Bender's own actions were a precipitating cause, but one especially cantankerous member made himself highly obnoxious at a business meeting and, after everyone had dispersed, phoned the pastor at home to carry on the feuding. Hardly had he begun his tirade when the line went ominously dead. Bender called back, only to discover that the caller had died suddenly of a heart attack. The event had an immensely quieting effect on future church business meetings and, in fact, added a measure of holy awe to church services. There were rededications and baptisms and some increase of membership. Helga, the pastor's youngest, who finished her eighth grade and then joined brothers Carl Ronald and Armin at Ravenswood High School, made her profession of faith and was baptized by her father after a somewhat active fling as a teenager. She had won a school popularity contest, sung in the high school trio and glee club, and been active in other student affairs, but now helped in the church's primary department.

Erica meanwhile did housework for room and board while she pursued, as already indicated, nurse's training and taught piano part-time. It was known that she felt called to missionary service and would go to Cameroon whenever the opportunity arose. A church member, Lambert Karst, sought to marry her, but she declined because he had no missionary call.

In 1929, ten years after the end of World War I, post-War conditions in the Cameroons—now entirely under British and French control—had settled to the degree that the missions director in Germany urged Bender to return for a three-year term in Soppo, the chief center of the British area. It was decided that Mother Bender would stay with Helga, still in high school, but that

Erica, now a graduate nurse, would go to Africa with her father. They would travel not aboard a freighter taking four weeks but by passenger ship. While in Europe they would report to the Berlin Missions headquarters and would also stop briefly at the home of Mother Bender's family near Dresden, where in 1904 on his first furlough from missionary service in Africa, Bender had married Hedwig Kloeber.

Bender was not the first missionary to return to Soppo, but he was the first American missionary to do so; in fact, British and French authorities permitted few missionaries of any kind to go back. Prior to Bender's return all missions affairs in pre-War Kamerun were channeled through Berlin's German Baptist Mission Society headquarters. British and French occupation had now closed that door. The Versailles Treaty and its Allied mandates system now regulated affairs for the British and French sectors. Bender now in 1929 would assume a key role in overcoming the exclusion of German foreign missions operations in the Cameroons. This he did by being processed and supported for his work in an independent sort of manner by the North American Baptist Missionary Society with offices in Forest Park, Illinois.

Both Bender and his daughter Erica worked tirelessly in Soppo and in outlying areas. Erica became physically exhausted, however, and after an unidentified experience of shock and trauma at one of the missions outposts, began to show psychic strain as well. It was thought best, therefore, that she return home several months early, at which time she then married Lambert Karst, still a leading member of Gross Park Immanuel Baptist Church. For all that, her condition worsened. Despite many efforts to restore her to good health, Erica lingered in hospital confinement until her death.

Meanwhile, with only part of a year remaining of his three-year term, and knowing that his wife and Helga and other family members were in Chicago, and that Erica's husband would be solicitously helpful, Bender maintained a strenuous double load of work in Africa before returning to the United States in 1932.

Later that same year, however, came an urgent appeal from the Berlin Mission. Missionary Hofmeister, a good friend of Bender, and only recently allowed return to Cameroon, was seriously ill and needed replacement. With the encouragement and blessing of the American German Baptist Mission Society Carl, and this time, Hedwig Bender were soon once again en route to Cameroon.

That last year in Chicago, 1932, was Helga's first year at Wheaton College in Wheaton, Illinois. Rather than living in Wheaton on campus she went there by train from Chicago every day. To catch the 6:30 a.m. that got her to college in time for pre-classes Missions Prayer Meeting, she was up for breakfast by 5:30. Bender then walked her daily to the train stop to assure a safe connection. After several months of this morning procedure Bender would be saying and waving her a last goodbye. Her next greeting from him awaits in heaven.

The Bender Family
in Chicago

18

SOPPO 1932–1935

Bender had never given up the hope and expectation of long-range return to Cameroon. He viewed the post-War years in America as an important interlude for developing family cohesion which was essentially realized by the end of the Watertown years. During this period he also remained in contact with his African workers, some of whom he had ordained for ministry and leadership.

His return to Africa in 1929–32 with daughter Erica thus realized his hope of once again being among the people and in the country that he loved. Much of this three-year period involved restoring the Soppo area from war-related devastation and post-war neglect. While buildings and gardens needed refurbishing to attractive usefulness, more than external renewal was especially essential. Internal strife among church members, the return of some to pagan beliefs and practices, the impact of foreign so-called prophets all threatened and confused Christian witness and work.

The reestablishment of Sunday schools as a special part of Erica's endeavors besides her women's work and health care, resumption of teachers' conferences, upgrading of church and business records, attention to schools, and launching of a prison ministry all combined to renew peoples' Christian dedication and participation. They were so happy, actually so excited about the missionaries' restorations, innovations, and spiritual shepherding that they voluntarily expressed a special resolution of appreciation.

Another strengthening factor during this term was the 1931 arrival at Soppo of Paul Gebauer, one of whose first assignments by Bender was repairing the roof of the mission house. This is mentioned with a smile in view of Gebauer's eventual thirty years of ministry, many of them as no-nonsense superintendent and administrator of the entire Cameroon Baptist work. When he went to the States on his first furlough and was denied an exit visa to return to Cameroon, Gebauer enlisted as a United States Army chaplain. At this juncture the German-headquartered phase of Cameroon work was turned over to the American mission board. This ended the troublesome arrangement between German and American mission boards that had functioned by bits and pieces since 1891, when American August Steffens and his successors including Bender were sent to Africa by a German board but were related as well to American supporters. With this organizational change the Gebauers as well as other Americans were now able to go unhindered to Cameroon.

Bender had given Gebauer two bits of advice: "Don't return to Cameroon under the German society's appointing," and "Don't come back single." Gebauer met both suggestions, and in addition to strong evangelistic zeal came equipped with sociological, socio-cultural, and comparative religions interests. While Bender was a student and writer about Duala and Bakwiri peoples, Gebauer more thoroughly highlighted sociological and anthropological concerns. This did not trouble Bender as it did some other missionaries. The two men worked well together exploring the Grasslands, among other things, where Gebauer would soon concentrate his efforts and where several of Bender's Soppo-trained seminarians would locate for church planting and evangelism.

Before long, another mission work impacting factor would be World War II. When Hitler threatened to control all Europe, British authorities interned all German missionaries in Cameroon and removed them to Jamaica. Thereupon, with the United States Baptist Mission board now already free to send its own workers overseas, and Gebauer being an inspiring representative of the same, many candidates—twenty-two in all, George and Louise Dunger and Laura Reddig among them—were soon in Cameroon. New churches were organized, church members increased, and school enrollments grew. The work underwent notable expansion.

Our story now backtracks to the Benders, who left the States in 1933 for what would unknowingly be their last term together in Cameroon, and who, though they had helped spark the advance into the Grasslands, would have but limited on-site ministry there. From a farewell service in Chicago the Benders held missionary rallies before actual departure for Hamburg. In New York son Herbert bade them farewell and presented them with a large bouquet of roses and a camera. Boarding ship in Hamburg on February 21, 1933, they arrived in Victoria on March 9. Fellow passengers included Presbyterian, Catholic, and Basel Mission workers, all like the Benders returning to their Cameroon ministries.

Welcoming parties were on hand for everyone. For the Benders it was Paul Gebauer who had borrowed an automobile and who in ninety minutes transported the

Benders effortlessly to Soppo, thus sparing them the all-too-familiar seven-hour trek.

Among the Benders' first check-ins and contacts in Soppo were to government officials, their trained teaching and preaching helpers, to all the welcoming parishioners, and to the school and its students that Bender had shaped to British requirements but with significant inclusion as well of biblical content. Hedwig had not been on the field during that major operation. Bender had instituted a thoroughgoing curriculum minus extraneous subjects. He had also included biblical instruction as foundational to character and citizenship building. Under this program, with 310 students enrolled in the British division and 30 in the Duala-speaking group, the Soppo school was now a model for all Baptist Mission education. Additionally, under Bender's preaching, teaching, and pastoral attention, many people had been converted; many had also learned carpentry, bricklaying, and principles of farming.

Hedwig rejoiced in what she saw. She also greeted well-remembered Cameroonians even as they cheered her return, and easily resumed responsibilities for church involvement and visitation, women's work, health care, and domestic duties. Now she would partner with Bender in implementing plans for a new church building to accommodate the growing church membership. Baptist believers in the extended Soppo area now numbered 2,000, more than the total count of three Grassland congregations. Mission officials pushed for the Benders to extend their term until 1937. While Gebauer and other American missionaries were now coming and going under the exclusive aegis of the North American Baptist Mission, Bender would nonetheless finish out his own Cameroon endeavors with still some threads of attachment to former German co-workers and their successors. (German missionaries had been permitted to return to Cameroon beginning in 1927 after a period of imposed delay.)

Announcement and discussions about building a new church were soon exciting topics of conversation. Enlisting the help of school children in the project could only heighten readiness of their parents and other adults to share in the physical exertions involved. Certain basic decisions needed to be made, however, about the building site, of materials to be used and their delivery, and of general systematic procedures. To locate the church on a gentle rise at the far end of the greensward between the mission house and the backdrop shadow of Mt. Cameroon seemed just right. There, with access from every direction and in harmonious relationship to structures already in place, the church would invite ready use and benefit for one and all.

Experienced in drawing and reading blueprints and in general construction, Bender worked alongside several helpers but at day's end carefully by himself inspected and adjusted, if necessary, what had been accomplished. Each day school children were reminded to bring sand and stones from the nearby river bed and bank to the building site. Girls brought baskets of sand, boys baskets of stones. During the children's school hours others, mostly adults, took over the supply system. When enough material had been piled up, Bender planted a Christian flag atop the mound to announce that actual building could and would now begin.

He himself made frames for producing concrete bricks. Natives meanwhile worked in shifts carrying water, mixing cement, and laying the church foundation and the rising walls. On one side, as a cornerstone, Bender sculpted a scene of Jesus weeping over Jerusalem. He little realized that only too soon he would be buried at this symbolic location.

Bender had aimed by the end of 1935 to complete a church seating almost five hundred worshippers, have Paul Gebauer give a dedicatory address, and then return to America where Hedwig had just arrived a bit early to check on Erica's illness and also to secure much needed rest for her own dangerously exhausted self. Now almost a senior at college, Helga met her mother at Union Station in Chicago and took her to share lodgings in Wheaton, Illinois.

In Soppo meanwhile after strenuous days of church construction Bender, as he had always done, worked usually until midnight on correspondence and organizing mission records. By morning's light he was once again ready to resume construction tasks. By now most of the work was finished except for the steeple that would tower above the trees and whose bell would call hundreds to worship. This climactic task Bender reserved entirely for himself.

In a letter dated July 30, 1935, Bender wrote: "By all means I am going home next spring." This was already an extension of the earlier hope to go home by July, 1935. "The burden has been too heavy, and I am only keeping up now by sheer will power. Every day is a working day and there is no chance to recuperate and rest up. Last night I worked till midnight again. This has become quite the rule." Yet the mission directors wanted Bender to stay until 1937! The younger chaps had all returned home, some of them even early, and claimed their now recently promised pension arrangement. Hopefully, thought Bender, he, too, would be able to complete his service on the field and receive a retirement payment of $1800.

Reminding himself of the divine imperative that kept him going, he plastered the interior of the church during the rainy season and prepared stone slabs for the topmost section of the tower. "The heaviest work is done," he wrote; "the Lord willing we shall dedicate the new edifice at Christmas." When one of Bender's children suggested that so-called religious priorities could constitute parental neglect, Bender reminded him, "It is not our fault nor of our own volition that Ma and I became missionaries—you must blame God for that, for it was he who called us into his service." As an evidence of God's approval he noted: "I now have forty-four native helpers assisting me in my work in the Soppo and Balondo areas."

In November, two months before Bender expected to complete his final term in Cameroon, he was at work on the church roof when he suddenly collapsed and fell to the ground. No bones were broken and he seemed to rally well. Black water fever set in, however, and after several days of round-the-clock expert medical attention Bender nonetheless had no strength to survive.

The Forest Park office phoned Helga in Wheaton to say that Bender died November 10, 1935, of black water fever and asked her to convey the news to her mother. Needless to say, this was no easy task for Helga. At the same time there was thanksgiving that under the circumstances Hedwig was under loving care. Bender's last letter to Forest Park headquarters, received the day of his death, stated among other things as if by premonition: "In a few months I shall close my missionary activity. In looking back over many years that my wife and I were permitted to serve in Soppo, especially during the difficult War years, I can only give praise and thanks.... We began the work with thirty-five members.... Today we have thirty-six churches with about 1600 members, not counting the large number who have already joined the church triumphant.... I look forward with joy to a reunion with them in heaven."

Hundreds of natives, government officials and workers, and fellow missionaries came to pay their respects to *Sango* Bender. Six carpenters prepared a coffin, since Cameroon heat required interment within twenty-four hours. The final service took place at 4 p.m. on Monday, November 11, the very day a ship was sailing from Victoria to Germany, just as Bender planned to do in about a month. Attending the service were 1,000 Cameroonians from near and far, and sixty Europeans who arrived in sixteen automobiles. With German missionary Karl Pantzlau presiding, the service opened with the singing of "Nearer My God to Thee," the reading of Psalm 90, and prayer. Pantzlau preached briefly on Revelation 14:13: "Blessed are the dead who die in the Lord from henceforth; yea, saith the Spirit, that they may rest from their labors, and their works do follow them." In closing his remarks he said, "God buries his workers, but his work continues.... 'Thanks be to God who giveth us the victory through our Lord Jesus Christ.'" The manager of a nearby large plantation spoke in brief tribute, as did three representatives of native churches. After song and prayer the coffin was lowered into the gravesite at the church's cornerstone, where the Victoria church choir sang hymns. Subsequently inscribed on a simple wooden cross gravemarker were words adapted from 2 Timothy 4:7: "He fought a good fight, he finished his course, he kept the faith."

19

WHERE ARE THEY NOW ?

In the summer of 1940 Helga Bender and Carl F. H. Henry were married in the chapel of Northern Baptist Theological Seminary in Chicago, where Carl would become professor of theology and Helga adjunct teacher in Christian Education and seminary librarian. Carl's student pastorate would be at Humboldt Park German Baptist Church where some of the Benders had worshipped. The Henrys were delighted when in time Mother Bender came to live with them and grandmothered Paul and Carol Henry. She later joined them as well in Pasadena, California, where Carl became a founding professor and acting dean of Fuller Theological Seminary, and Helga as part of her community involvements taught at Pasadena College (now Point Loma College) as Associate Professor of Education. Those years were memorable as Paul and Carol gained strong spiritual roots in Christian schools and at Mission Covenant Church. Memories of Rose Bowl games and of New Year's Parades, not to mention the ins and outs of countless visitors at home, became indelible memories. It was a time as well when Carl spent a sabbatical at New College, Edinburgh, Scotland, and had his first trip to Asia and elsewhere as co-teacher/preacher with men like Bob Pierce, founder of World Vision.

Mother Bender was a happy participant and contributor to all this activity. The medical warning Helga had received about her mother's inoperable aneurism and which Helga kept secret from her came true in 1957. At her hospital bedside she shared a dream in which Carl Bender reached out to her with a lovely Christmas tree. For many earlier Germans the Christmas tree had symbolized celebration of the redeeming Savior's birth. With a smile on her face she closed her eyes as Carl offered the Aaronic benediction and Hedwig departed from this world.

Her funeral service and burial took place in Watertown, Wisconsin. In charge was brother-in-law Henry Schroeder, well-known North American Baptist pastor (as was his son) and husband of Carl Bender's sister, Helene. At the viewing Hedwig's hand rested on a Bible opened to one of her favorite passages, as a kind of admonition to everyone present: "... [T]hanks be to God, who giveth us the victory through our Lord Jesus Christ. Therefore my beloved brethren, be ye steadfast, unmovable, always abounding in the work of the Lord, forasmuch as ye know that your labor is not in vain in the Lord" (I Corinthians 15:57–58). All the children, including Herbert, attended the service. Carl Bender's well-worn Greek New Testament that Hedwig had carefully preserved was placed in Herbert's hands as a special token of his parents' love.

The believer's pilgrimage journey had not been easy or without detours for some of the Bender children, even though as part of the Benders' commitment to missionary calling they had in faith entrusted all their children to God's care and redeeming grace. For some that faith was confirmed sooner, for others later. What rejoicing it has been and will continue to be when all the Benders from diverse places and experiences are therefore reunited in their heavenly Father's Welcome Home embrace. Meeting them as well will be sojourners from Africa, Europe, the United States, and elsewhere to exult in hallelujahs for what God has done, and continues to do for "whosoever will."

Hedwig Bender is buried in Oak Hill Cemetery, Watertown, Wisconsin, where sons Herbert and Thorwald are also interred, as well as several of Thorwald's children.

Erica Bender Karst was buried in Chicago after a Moody Memorial Church service arranged by her husband. Carl Ronald's body was taken to his wife's family plot in Missouri. Still living are Armin Bender and Helga Bender Henry. Armin continues to live in Rochester, New York, a community he never left after university days except for World War II service which earned him a purple heart. The Oak Hill Watertown plot reserved for Helga and her husband Carl F. H. Henry has a gravestone inscribed "Friends of the King." The stone mason, alas, asked "What King?"

The graves of Valentin and Helene Wolff, long-time Bender associates in Cameroon and in Watertown-related ministries, are also at Oak Hill Cemetery. Wolff and Bender had in the 1890s in fact been students together at the Rochester, New York, German Baptist Seminary. The children of both families knew each other at the Children's Home in Germany. One of the Wolff sons who became a professional agriculturalist is buried in an adjoining community. During World War II near his birthplace in Kamerun his plane crashed or was shot down among people who saved him from bleeding to death. He would gladly have returned to them for some kind of ministry.

Of early Cameroon workers still living is Mrs. Gerda

Godt, nee Reimer, born in Kamerun in 1905. Her father Heinrich Reimer, educated at Hamburg Baptist Seminary and for medicine in London, and Gerda's mother, trained as a nurse in London, were good friends of the Benders. Gerda was the first and only child of Reimer's first wife who died of black water fever. After joining her father and a second wife on their honeymoon Gerda, age three, was left for care with a Hamburg family. Her second mother also died of black water fever and left two young sons. In 1914 when Heinrich Reimer with a third wife and two boys of the previous marriage arrived in Hamburg to now move Gerda to the Children's Home near Berlin, she met her third mother and her brothers for the first time. They were meeting Gerda for the first time as well. Because Reimer was conscripted for four years of Red Cross work, he and his family waited still longer before time together. This occurred in Argentina in connection with Reimer's pastorate there. Now eighteen years of age, Gerda met a missionary from Canada whom she subsequently married and with whom she worked for seven years with an interdenominational mission. When the Great Depression deterred missions operations, Gerda, now Gerda Godt, and her husband came to the United States where they ministered together happily until his death in 1983. After more than a decade as a widow active in church music and other efforts, Gerda now at ninety-three years of age is invalided with severe osteoarthritis. Surely her experience as a Missionary Kid (MK) with three mothers has been unique, as has also been the life of her father who maintained his excellent Kamerun ministry with the help of three wives, who each in their own way and lifespan were a part of Kamerun mission history.

The Rohdes, mentioned earlier, thrust penniless into British internment for a short time with the Benders at

Soppo, and then shipped to London, eventually returned to Australia. God graciously called one of their daughters and her husband, Dr. Edwin Tscharke, to forty-four years of unique ministry in New Guinea. Some of Tscharke's special medical books, some even in Pidgin English, have been shared with health workers presently engaged in Nigeria and Cameroon. The passing of a ministerial torch to children or grandchildren has been a unique gift of remembrance to pioneers long lost and forgotten in the thicket of subsequent history.

The same could be said of the George Dungers who, like Gebauer, in the inter-War period forged needed mission procedural changes and worked as well with Cameroonians who remain deeply thankful and indebted to them. Honoring the Lord, like her parents, Daphne Dunger although retired by illness from overseas work, has by her own strategic medical and evangelistic work been a tribute to parental influence and God's compelling call. To what extent is she ongoingly remembered?

Also not to be forgotten is Laura Reddig whose personal work among lepers, for example, and whose contagious influence helped bring many persons face to face with God's call to Cameroon. Honored by the Queen of England, Laura during years of final illness and death was all too briefly mentioned by missions-deficient and seemingly little interested people.

God be praised that he remembers and pronounces the "Well done" for good and faithful servants. As Matthew 25:14 and following reminds those who invest themselves for God, workers of all times and races and places long forgotten or being forgotten, rest in the incomparable joy of their Lord. Labors for Christ and his Kingdom, even unmarked or unknown graves of his messengers, are stamped with God's seal of eternal remembrance.

"Where Are They Now?" should include remembrance as well of Cameroonians who themselves and/or whose children and even grandchildren testify to the ministry of pioneer missionaries. Having lived in the Washington, D.C., area for over thirty years, Helga and Carl Henry met and entertained such people and had access to embassies and organizations active in African affairs. Blessed with a large home they gladly entertained internationals, among them Cameroonians for whom Washington was often a lonely place. Cameroon-related pictures and artifacts always stimulated both memories of their distant homes and loved ones, and ready conversation about personal hopes and problems.

The Henry guest book contains the names, among others, of E. K. and Mrs. Martin, their sons Carmichael and Samuel, M.D.; Emanuel Burnley, Stephen Nteff and two daughters, Daniel Ekiko, M. T. Kima of the Embassy and his Soppo wife Frieda, and Soppo Chief Monono's son. Pamela Martin we met at the Embassy. Other Cameroonian ambassadorial people we met in Holland at the Hague International Church, of whom one wife had been a Soppo student. This is mentioned simply to emphasize that African missions-related individuals are to be found in various places for befriending and also for learning something of the impact Christian witness made in times past.

Another Cameroonian met in the Washington area is Félicité Kuoh whose interest in the Henrys and in this present book merit special mention. Born in Cameroon and for many years a member of the Ivory Coast Embassy staff she, as many Washingtonians do for Saturday relaxation, drove to the suburbs for perhaps a stop or two at frequent estate or garage sales.

On just such a Saturday Félicité appeared in suburban Arlington to browse at a Henry sale. When Helga noticed her lengthy study of some not-for-sale items she struck up a conversation with the young lady. Before long, since the visitor identified herself as from French Cameroun, she and Helga chatted over coffee for several hours and bonded into a special relationship. On periodic trips home to Cameroun Félicité therefore reported to Helga about Soppo, took pictures, and even visited several native Baptist veterans in Victoria to augment information she had found in the booklet *Bender in the Cameroons*.

Her and others' growing interest in establishing a library or museum of Cameroon history other than one about arts and crafts keeps Félicité alert to sources of information other than oral tradition. The Allies' deliberate destruction of valuable books and records during World War I created a dearth of both tribal and colonial information now difficult to recover. Increased numbers of educated nationals are therefore now researching and writing to fill in blanks in their heritage.

One way to secure such knowledge is to examine and compile ancestral data. In doing this Félicité has supplied the following, for example, that is significant not only for her and her people but also for successor witnesses. Thus she herself becomes someone to be remembered but becomes also a key to those who are trying to define and minister within their own history.

"My *grandfather* Manga," she reports, was a student and convert at the Duala boarding school of the early 1900s. Later he was a teacher there, and also became a pastor of a Duala Baptist Church.

"My *grandmother* Jacqueline Ndolo Ekolo, a princess, was a student at the Duala Girls' School that is still functioning today.

"*Grandfather* named his youngest daughter *Soppo* and his first son *Duala*. This is not by accident or coincidence. *Duala* is where he, grandfather, 'received Christ.' *Soppo* is the place where he knew he could always find the Bender people in communion with God, a place of spiritual inner strength.

"Son Duala's other name was *Valentin*—probably after Valentin Wolff who served in Cameroon during the same period.

"Your father [Bender] is clearly responsible for my grandfather's Christian education and conversion to Christianity. And therefore he is also partly responsible for me and my whole family being members of the Christian Baptist Church of Cameroon ever since."

Testimonials of this kind validate missions and missionaries of earlier times that may be easily forgotten. They also call us to remember those around us who lack and need Christian commitment and connection. "Where Are They Now?" honors those who are in heaven with their missions accomplished. "Where Are They Now?" refers as well to those yet available to forge intergenerational links of Christian witness at home and abroad.

Missionary impact has transformed not only many thousands of Cameroon natives and families, but in some cases even entire villages and tribes. Tens of thousands of churches, some admittedly in need of trained pastors, are being effectively nurtured by the seminary in Ndu. There, encouraged by the African theological accrediting association ACTEA, more and more of the faculty have Master's degrees and a few have earned doctorates.

Cameroon hospitals remain the best in the country. Banso Baptist Hospital has an eye-surgery wing unique in Cameroon, and the leprosy ward in Mbingo Baptist Hospital is in the forefront of leprosy care.

20

MT. CAMEROON REVISITED

The purpose of Bender's first ascent and return from Mt. Cameroon in 1909 was to assure the Bakwiris of the non-existence of killer evil spirits. Their astute even wily tradespeople used selfishly guarded east-to-west-and-reverse market routes, of course, but at lower mountain levels. Natives who ventured to upper reaches, despite skeletons and skulls along the way, did so primarily as porters for whites who depended on them to carry food and other supplies, to scout terrain, to cope with animals, to intervene if necessary in tribal encounters, and in case of emergencies to be foot-fleet messengers for help.

Towering behind Soppo and visible for miles from all directions the almost 14,000-foot volcanic mountain had for centuries teased for examination. Early Atlantic seamen spoke of fire flares in its craggy heights and palls of smoke drifting earthward. As far as most Africans were concerned it defied serious exploration. Their tribal religions, in fact, inherently warned against doing so.

Many whites, on the other hand, considered Mt. Cameroon a worthy challenge. Among them, scientists, agronomists, hunters, and even colonial affiliates envisioned accolades for being the first person to discover this or that, and for this or that purpose. The fact that it seldom divulged all its secrets, certainly not all at once, kept increasing numbers of variously motivated venturers heeding her summons.

After a ten-year span in Soppo, Bender's ascent was unrelated to self-aggrandizing purposes. Under God's gracious governance Hedwig and he had hung on through the roller-coaster pre-during-and-post-War I highs and lows of mission work. It was now time, before an inevitable clamor of farewells, for quiet and private thanksgiving to him from whom had indeed flowed every blessing of safety, provision, and endurance.

By this time Bender's feet and legs could almost automatically find their way to Buea. At about 3,000 feet above sea level, it had for beneficent health reasons outclassed historic Duala. Here an assortment of German and later British officials had issued travel passes, filed passports or other authenticating materials for Bender, and all in all had played watch dog over Kamerun people and affairs.

Its beautiful villas, tree-lined avenues, and cultural heritage of the Alfred Saker era in both Dualaland and Victoria became, slavery reminder remnants notwithstanding, a choice boost to German enlargement after 1884. Here Governor Jesko von Puttkamer built his regal residence, here plantation tycoons and other plutocrats whiled away their terms of office. But here, too, as Bender recalled as he now climbed, early Basel and later Baptist churches and schools left their mark on successive generations. Going to Buea for whatever reason was indeed usually capitol professional business but no less a place of Christian witness and influence.

Another approximately 3,000 feet of climbing brought Bender at 6,000 feet above sea level to a cinchona plantation that he saw established during his first Soppo years. The medical bark of its trees supplied quinine, essential not only in the tropics but also elsewhere for curbing or treating malaria. When properly prescribed and used by the Benders what a life-saving substance it became! Many of their co-workers had succumbed to malaria's frequent spawn, namely, black water fever. Surely the Benders' own physical well-being not to mention the restorative treatment of guests at their Soppo Rest Center witnessed to the Great Physician's ever-ready presence and help. No doubt on this self-imposed climb up Mt. Cameroon Bender was well supplied with quinine, perhaps even home-grown!

The next stop from Musaka, the cinchona plantation, would be Hut Number One. So far the hike from Soppo had been through primary and secondary forest, thickets of various ferns including tree ferns hundreds of feet high, and clumps of white mushrooms under foot. Near a rest bungalow a sudden drop of ten feet to a lava cave brought to sight bats and decomposed animal bones. Seeming paths led to a small lake. Scottish heather had accompanied him much of the way, and small animals scattered at his coming. Butterflies and huge moths lit here and there.

Forests the next morning suddenly opened to bare, slippery grassland where an almost perpendicular climb up a cone-shaped hill revealed remains of a former hut. Across a stony plateau that followed stood a corrugated iron hut with a long sloping inside shelf for sleeping. Here was an opportunity as well to build a fire and to eat and savor carefully bottled water.

As in 1909, Bender once again made it to about 12,000 feet above sea level, but not to the mountain top with its gaping half-mile wide crater. Wisdom was calling for descent back to Buea and Soppo. Heavy fog had settled in, and the winds were powerful enough to sweep unwary climbers into yawning holes. Just one further thing needed doing, however—checking the hut's tourist register that might reveal growing interest for climbing Mt. Cameroon and by whom. Indeed, among signees were members of the Cameroon Alpine Society, as well as government officials, missionaries, merchants, and plantation people. Whether Bender added his name awaits someone else's report.

Much more significant for Bender in this climb with its memories and associations of times past was what he now saw below rather than above him. As storm clouds lifted and the sun broke through, a beautiful rainbow arched across his beloved country and its people.

Generally speaking the biblical rainbow of Genesis 9 symbolizes something of God's and man's interrelationships. Worship and blessing go hand in hand.

With retirement before him in 1919 Bender surely longed to remind his people and personally demonstrate that faithful obedience to and worship of the Lord who daily calls and equips his children for life and work, are what bring wise blessings for all to enjoy. He often wrestled with questions like the following and hoped to stimulate contagious interest among other missionaries and especially among his trainees and church people to seek and implement valid answers.

—How cruelly and sadly tribal and world warfare ravages families, schools, churches, and governments! Will and how can natives and citizens elsewhere learn and practice principles and paths of righteousness that lead to God-blessed peace?

—Comfortable compromise with cultural and social evils has diluted, even eradicated years of hard-won steadfastness in upright behavior. Will and how can

stronger contenders for what is right lovingly yet firmly
help restore their erring fellows?

—Increased intrusion of false religions threatens the
strength and testimony of fearless biblical commitment.
How can Christianity be saved from creeping takeover?

—Deliberate slavery to or the allurement of current
evil practices leads to personal and transmitted
self-destruction. How can Christians thwart inevitable
racial and community suicide?

Bender's concerns over such encroaching problems
often initiated by deliberate schemes or personal practices
of ungodly whites and others had always troubled him. He
was aware, also of course, of worldwide pervading evil
powers and loyalties. In the last analysis, as his
seminarians, school children, church and family members,
and in fact everyone must be reminded, only by God's
saving grace and indwelling Spirit, and by submission to
his power and safekeeping, can and will satanic forces be
overcome.

As Bender gazed through the rainbow climax of his
mountain climb he saw Cameroon's entire landscapes
—north, south, east, west, and even beyond. He
personally practiced and taught his people not only
Kamerun-, but also globe-encircling, prayer as part of
world neighbor love and evangelism.

Bender was often weary of body but not of
commitment to God's call. His conviction, moreover, that
blacks should and would some day lead their people and
countries into authentic independence for their own and
others' spiritual enlightenment never left him.

With retirement soon at hand, he, as well as Hedwig,
recognized the need of transmitting a deeper meaning of
his comment, "I shall not die but declare the Word of the
Lord." In 1899 he had been queried about his possible

physical unlikelihood of surviving the rigors of early Africa. It became a challenge not limited to the Benders but also to other workers. They saw in others around them, as God's blessing of faith, converts and trained co-workers assuming responsibilities. Now it was time to increasingly transfer mantles not only of work but also of God's motivation and conviction to nationals to carry forward the task of worldwide Christian enterprise from generation to generation.

He and Hedwig envisioned that great Day of the Lord when missionaries of all times together with their spiritual children would gather with him, the Giver not only of earth's fleeting peace but also of his receivable eternal peace that, even now, passes understanding.

WRITINGS BY C. J. BENDER

African Jungle Tales. Little Blue Book, No. 561. Girard,
Kansas: Haldeman-Julius Company, 1920s.

Beleedi ba Eyal' a Loba (teachings from the Word of God),
Kassel: J. G. Oncken Nachfolger, 1932.

Bible Studies (clippings written for *Der Sendbote* from
Watertown, 1921–1925)

Dubuise la Bosangi, kapenda beleedi ba Eyal' a Loba, Kassel,
Oncken Press.

Diary, handwritten records of receipts and expenditures
related to ministry in Kamerun from 1914 to 1932,
including record of materials sent to African workers
from Watertown and Chicago.

Kamerun Blätter und Skizzen. Kassel: J. G. Oncken
Nachfolger, 1927.

Lebensfragen I. *Die gröszte aller Fragen:* "Was dünket euch
um Christo?", Stuttgart, Druck von Lämmle u.
Müllerschön, n.d.

Mokusa's Tochter, a mission story written for *Der Sendbote*
in 1928 during Bender's ministry in Chicago.

Muleedi, teachers' guide handwritten in Duala in Great
Soppo dated Jan.-Feb., 1931 and May-June, 1934.

Poetry. Handwritten in English and German, unpublished,
many items reflecting on historical events or on his
travels.

Proverbs of West Africa. Little Blue Book, No. 505. Girard, Kansas: Haldeman-Julius Company, 1924.

Religious and Ethical Beliefs of African Negroes: Duala and Wakweliland. Little Blue Book, No. 798. Girard, Kansas, Haldeman-Julius Company, 1925.

Thoughts on Jesus the Christ and Christianity. Handwritten in English. 65 pgs., n.d.

Twenty Years Among African Negroes. Little Blue Book, No.797. Girard, Kansas: Haldeman-Julius Company, 1925.

Die Volksdichtung der Wakweli: Sprichwörter Febeln und Märchen, Parabelen, Rätsel und Lieder. Introd. by J. Ipsen. Berlin: Dietrich Reimer, A.-G., 1922.

Der Weltkrieg und die christlichen Missionen in Kamerun. Kassel: J. C. Oncken Nachfolger, 1921.

(Additionally correspondence directed by Bender to the Baptist mission directors during his terms of service is useful.)

BIBLIOGRAPHY

Ardener, Shirley, *Eye-Witnesses to the Annexation of Cameroon 1883–1887*. Buea, Cameroon Government Press, 1968.

Ardener, Shirley, and Warmington, W. A., *Plantation and Village in the Cameroons*. London, Oxford University Press, 1960.

Ayandele, E. A., *The Missionary Impact on Modern Nigeria, 1842–1914* (A Political and Social Analysis), Evanston, Northwestern University Press, n.d.

Baillie, Albert Victor, *My First Eighty Years*, London, John Murray, 1951.

Balders, Günter, *100 Jahre Mission in Kamerun*, Berlin 1991 conference report.

Bender, Erica, Diary (with German and English entries beginning in 1916 and extending to 1931).

——*The Handbook on First Aid in the British Cameroons*, with German additions by Erica's mother Hedwig Bender, and laundry hints by Anne Gebauer.

Buell, Raymond Leslie, *The Native Problem in Africa*, New York, The Macmillan Press, 1928.

Burke, Fred, ed., Africa, *Selected Readings*, Boston, Houghton Mifflin Co., n.d.

Calvert, Albert F., *The Cameroons*, London, T. Werner Laurie Ltd., 1917.

Cary, Joyce, *Britain and West Africa*. London, Longmans, Green and Co., 1946.

Clarke, Peter B., *West Africans at War, 1914–18, 1939–45*. Colonial Propaganda and Its Cultural Aftermath. London, Ethnographica,1986.

Dominik, Hans, *Vom Atlantik zum Tschadsee, Kriegs und Forschungsfahrten in Kamerun*. Berlin, Ernst Siegfried 20 Mittler und Sohn, 1908.

Drummond, Lewis, *Spurgeon: Prince of Preachers*. Grand Rapids, Kregel, 1992.

Elango, Lovett Z., *Britain and Bimbia in the Nineteenth Century, 1833 -1878, A Study in Anglo-Bimbian Trade and Diplomatic Relations*. Ph.D. dissertation at Boston University, 1974.

Fage, J. D., *An Introduction to the History of West Africa*. Cambridge, England, University Press, 1966.

Farwell, Byron, *The Great War in Africa, 1914–1918*. New York, W. W. Norton & Co, n.d.

Fetter, Bruce, ed., *Colonial Rule in Africa*. Readings From Primary Sources. University of Wisconsin Press, 1979.

Fraser, Donald, *The Future of Africa*. Westport, Connecticut, Negro Universities Press, 1970.

Fuller, Harold, *People of the Mandate*. The story of the World Evangelical Fellowship. Grand Rapids, Baker 1996.

Gann, L. H., and Duignan, Peter, *The Rulers of German Africa*. Stanford University Press, 1997.

Gifford, Prosser and Louis, William Roger, eds., *Britain and Germany in Africa*. Imperial Rivalry and Colonial Rule. New Haven, Yale University Press.

Gorges, E. Howard, *The Great War in West Africa*. By the commandant of the West African Regiment. London, Hutchison & Co., 1930.

Grey, Viscount Edward of Fallowdon, *Twenty-Five Years*

1892–1916. New York, Frederick A. Stokes Company, 1925.

Groves, C. P., *The Planting of Christianity in Africa,* vols. 2 and 3. London, Lutterworth Press, 1955.

Günther, Jürgen, *Mission in kolonialen Kontext.* (dissertation). Hamburg University, 1985.

Hallett, Robin, *Africa Since 1875.* Ann Arbor, University of Michigan Press, 1974.

Hargreaves, John D., *Prelude to the Partition of West Africa.* New York, St. Martin Press, 1966.

Historical Section of the Foreign Office–Cameroon. No. 118. Confidential. Xeroxed at the School of Oriental and African Studies, London.

Jenkins, Paul. *Guide to the Basel Mission's Cameroon Archive.* Basel, 1988.

Johnston, Sir Harry H., *A History of the Colonization of Africa.* New York, Cooper Square Publishers, Inc., 1966.

Kiessling, Elmer C. *Watertown Remembered.* Milwaukee, Wisconsin, Franklin Publishers, Inc., 1976.

Kürenberg, Joachim von, *The Kaiser: A Life of Wilhelm II, Last Emporer of Germany* (translated by H. T. Russell and Herta Hagen.) New York, Simon and Schuster, 1955.

Kwast, Lloyd Emerson, *The Discipling of West Cameroon.* Grand Rapids, Eerdmans, 1971.

——*The Origins and Nineteenth Century Development of Protestant Christianity in West Cameroon.* Doctor of Missiology thesis, Fuller Theological Seminary, 1972.

Latourette, Kenneth Scott, *The Expansion of Christianity,* Vol VII. Advance Through Storm, A.D. 1914 and After. New York, Harper & Brothers, 1945.

——*A History of Christianity.* New York, Harper & Brothers, 1953.

Nkwi, Paul Nchoji and Jean-Pierre Warnier, *Elements for a History of the Western Grassfields*. University of Yaoundi, Department of Sociology, 1982.

Meister, Jakob, *Bericht über den Kongresz der Europaischen Baptisten 26.- 31. Juli 1958 in Berlin*. Kassel, J. G. Oncken Verlag, 1959.

Migeod, Frederick William High, *Through British Cameroons*. London, Heath Cranton Ltd., 1925.

Missions-Bibellese-Kalender, 1914 through 1920. Annual Bible study readings and short articles. Berlin, German Baptist Mission Society.

Der Neuruppiner Missionsbote, F. W. Simoleit, ed., monthly pamphlets issued by the Mission Society of Berlin.

Noble, Frederic Perry, *The Redemption of Africa*. A story of Civilization. New York, Fleming H. Revell Company, 1899.

Northcott, Cecil, *Christianity in Africa*. London, SCM Press Ltd., 1963.

Norwood, Frederick A., *The Development of Modern Christianity Since 1500*. New York, Abingdon Press, 1956.

Puttkamer, Jesko von, *Gouverneurs Jahre in Kamerun*. Berlin, Georg Stilke, 1912.

Ramaker, Albert, *Eine kurze Geschichte der Baptisten*. Cleveland, Verlagshaus der deutschen Baptisten, 1906.

Rudin, Harry, *Germans in the Cameroons, 1884–1914*. New Haven, Yale University Press, 1938.

Saker, E. M., *Alfred Saker. Pioneer of the Cameroons*. London, The Carey Press, 1929.

Scheve, Eduard, *Die Baptisten-Mission in Kamerun*. Kassel, 1891.

——*Blüthen und Früchte aus Kamerun, West Afrika*, Berlin, 1894–1896.

——*Die Mission der deutschen Baptisten in Kamerun (von 1884–1901)*. Kassel, n.d.

Schlatter, Wilhelm, *Die Geschichte der Basler Mission in Afrika*. Verlag der Basler Missionsbuchhandlung, 1916.

Schneider, G., *Go: A graphic portrayal of a Christian mission at work in the Cameroons, West Africa*. Forest Park, North American Baptist General Conference, 1957.

Schreiber, August Wilhelm, ed., *Kameruner Kriogsorlebnisse in deutscher und englischer Beleuchtung; Antworten* der deutschen Baptisten missionare Valentin Wolff und Wilhelm Märtens auf das englische Blaubuch von November 15. Gütersloh, Germany, C. Bertelsmann 1917.

Seidel, A., *Deutsch-Kamerun, Wie es ist und was es verspricht*. Berlin, Verlag Meidinger, 1906.

Stark, W., *The Martyrdom of the Evangelical Missionaries in Cameroon 1914* (Reports of Eyewitnesses). Berlin-Steglitz, 1915.

Steiner, P., *Kamerun als Kolonie und Missionsfeld*. Basel, Verlag der Basler Missionsbuchhandlung, 1909.

Stoeker, H., *Kamerun unter deutscher Kolonialherrschaft, East Berlin*. Band I, 1960. Band II, 1968. Verlag der Wissenschaften, Humboldt University.

Student, Erich, *Deutsche Tat im Weltkrieg 1914–18*. Berlin, Verlag Bernard & Graefe.

Thomas, Anna Braithwaite and others. *St. Stephen's House, Friends Emergency Work in England 1914 to 1920*. Emergency Committee for the Assistance of Germans, Australians and Hungarians in Distress. London, n.d.

Townsend, Mary Evelyn, *The Rise and Fall of Germany's Colonial Empire 1844–1918*. New York, The Macmillan Co., 1930.

Turner, Harold W., *Religious Innovation in Africa*. Collected Essays on New Religious Movements. Boston, G. K.

Hall & Co., 1979.

Underhill, Edward Bean, *Alfred Saker*. Missionary to Africa. London, The Carey Kingsgate Press, 1884.

Weber, Charles W., *International Influences and Baptist Mission in West Cameroon*. German-American Missionary Endeavor under International Mandate and British Colonialism, Leiden, E. J. Brill, 1993.

Woyke, Frank H., *Heritage and Ministry of the North American Baptist Conference*, North American Baptist Conference, Oakbrook Terrace, Illinois, 1979.

ADDITIONAL SOURCES

Basel Mission Archives, Basel, Switzerland

Official Reports, about 50 largely in German, pertaining to Kamerun

Hamburg German Baptist Seminary Archives, Hamburg, Germany

Monthly periodicals, pre- and post-War, pertaining to Kamerun

*****Unsere Heidenmission*

*****Wahrheitszeuge*

Personal Correspondence

INDEX

Alle´grot, 83, 122
All-evangelicals Conference, 73 f,
American German Baptists, 37 f., 137
American Presbyterians, 81
American Tract Society, 19
Archives,   2, 44
Artist,   8, 14, 142

191